HENRY WILLIAMSON
THE MAN, THE WRITINGS

Essays by
Sylvia Bruce
Alexandra Burgess
Hugh Cecil
Kerstin Hegarty
David Hoyle
Ted Hughes
Oswald Jones
E. W. Martin
Roger Mortimore
Diana Mosley
Brocard Sewell
&
Ruth Tomalin
with an Introduction by Ronald Duncan

Edited by
Brocard Sewell
with two essays by Henry Williamson
an address by Ted Hughes
and poems by Sylvia Bruce
and Trevor Hold

Henry Williamson, by Rose Marie Duncan

HENRY WILLIAMSON THE MAN, THE WRITINGS

A Symposium

TABB HOUSE
Padstow, Cornwall

Printed in Great Britain by
T. J. Press (Padstow) Ltd,
Padstow, Cornwall.
Binding by Robert Hartnoll Ltd,
Bodmin, Cornwall.

FOREWORD

THE IDEA OF THIS BOOK was conceived after Henry Williamson's funeral, at Georgeham, in North Devon, on the afternoon of 18 August 1977, as old friends stood in his field at Ox's Cross, talking and thinking of him while ancient sunlight fell on them and warmed them. As a result, seven friends who knew him well have set down their memories of him, together with their reflections on aspects of his life and work. To these essays there have been added contributions by Sylvia Bruce and Hugh Cecil, on Williamson's nature writings and his writings on the Great War, and an essay by Roger Mortimore on *A Chronicle of Ancient Sunlight*. As far as I know, this is the first critical survey of Williamson's huge novel-sequence in its entirety. To complete the book there are reprinted two articles by Henry Williamson, written respectively in 1957 and 1970, which were first published in two magazines, one British, the other Canadian, of small circulation.[1] In these essays Williamson reflects on his motives for writing, and on the directions his life and thought had taken over the years. To these are added the text of Mr Ted Hughes's address at the memorial service at St Martin-in-the-Fields on 1 December 1977.

For some of the contributors, to write of Henry Williamson with complete fairness has been a difficult task. With so controversial a personality, as he seemed to many, it cannot have been easy to achieve a balance and avoid distortion. Inevitably, some of the contributors see the same things, but see them differently. To some of them Williamson is a complex personality, difficult to decipher; to others, all his actions become explicable in the light of a certain fundamental simplicity.

Similarly with regard to Williamson's works; at least one contributor agrees with those critics who have judged his best books to be his nature books: notably *Tarka the Otter* and *Salar the Salmon*; perhaps with the short early war book *The Patriot's Progress*, so much admired by Arnold Bennett and T. E. Lawrence, as runner-up. Others agree with John Middleton Murry and George D. Painter in acclaiming the long novel-series *A Chronicle of Ancient Sunlight* as his masterpiece. Another would award that title to *The Flax of Dream*, and in particular to *The Beautiful Years* or *Dandelion Days*, the latter being one of the best novels of schooldays in the language. As long ago as 1931 the late Waveney Girvan had said, in the introduction to his *A Bibliography and a Critical Survey of the Works of Henry Williamson*, that 'The novel has been his most successful mode of expression and it is evident that he is, and will be, pre-eminently a novelist.'

Two of Williamson's former secretaries, Alexandra Burgess and Kerstin Hegarty, contribute short memoirs which constitute valuable personal witness. The first part of Mrs Burgess's contribution was written in 1958, and was first published in a small book of which only 450 copies were printed,[2] where it appeared under her maiden name. The second part was written in June 1978. Mrs Hegarty's essay is very slightly adapted from the text of a recorded talk that was heard at a literary conference in 1969. It has not been previously published. The author has also taken the opportunity to incorporate a few suggestions made by Henry Williamson after he had read the original typescript, the principal one being the passage about Williamson's dog, Robbie.

For permission to quote from the works of Henry Williamson, and from his letters, I am indebted to Mr Richard Williamson; and to Mrs Anne Williamson I am grateful for helpful advice. My thanks are also due to Mr

Oswald Jones for making available his photographs of Henry Williamson, and to Gabriel Bergonzi for her valuable editorial assistance.

Mr Trevor Hold has kindly allowed me to present his poem 'Ancient Sunlight', which has not previously been published, within the context of my own contribution.

The contributors to this volume have been most patient with editorial insistencies and delays; and I greatly value the kindness of Mr Ronald Duncan in writing the introduction and of Mrs Duncan in providing the frontispiece, from her 1951 drawing of Henry Williamson, now in the possession of Mrs Kerstin Hergarty, to whom also grateful thanks are due.

Special thanks are due to Ted Hughes, and Olwyn Hughes, for permission to reprint Mr Hughes's obituary tribute to Henry Williamson; also to Sylvia Bruce for her kindness in correcting the proofs with such nicety; and to Caroline White, of Tabb House, for her patient care in the book's production.

Brocard Sewell

NOTES

1. Henry Williamson, 'Some Notes on "The Flax of Dream" and "A Chronicle of Ancient Sunlight" ', in *The Aylesford Review*, vol. ii, no. 2, Winter 1957-8; and 'An Affirmation', in *The Antigonish Review,* vol. i, no. 1 (St. Francis Xavier University, Antigonish, N.S.), Spring 1970.
2. Alexandra Wigginton, 'Henry Williamson', in *Frederick Rolfe and Others: A Miscellany of Essays* (Aylesford, St. Albert's Press, 1961).

CONTENTS

Photographs of Henry Williamson at Ox's Cross,
Aylesford Priory, Cannock Chase, on Exmoor,
and in London, by Oswald Jones

CONTENTS

Photographs of Henry Williamson at Ox's Cross,
Aylesford Priory, Cannock Chase, on Exmoor,
and in London, by Oswald Jones

LIST OF ILLUSTRATIONS

INTRODUCTION

I KNEW HENRY WILLIAMSON for forty years. But I cannot remember where we met. I think he had reviewed my *Journal of a Husbandman*, which Faber's had published during the war. Henry wrote at some length to congratulate me on this book. Perhaps he then just dropped in at my farm, as he continued to do, three or four times a year, until he died. We lived only forty miles apart.

We liked each other. It gives me considerable pleasure to write this little introduction to the collection of essays written by some of his friends.

Unhappily these were too few. And amongst his enemies, Henry himself would have to head the list: he took offence easily; and gave offence, readily. But unlike Evelyn Waugh, who cultivated rudeness, Henry did little more than tease. He was too sensitive of other people's feelings to hurt them deliberately. He was essentially a gentle man, being himself most vulnerable. Indeed, his whole life from the Somme onwards was one long wound.

I failed owing to my own ill-health to visit him in his final billet. But a friend went in my stead. I was not surprised to hear from him that Henry had talked wholly of the Somme. His life had been a repeated walk through that nightmare. He was not killed on that battlefield, but he was certainly maimed, crippled and wounded on it.

I admired Henry as a writer because he had an internal vision, was dedicated to the craft, and was not a pot-boiling journalist. And, more importantly, because he had a microscopic eye and could produce the accurate image. For example, his observation that the salmon's skin was like 'new cut pewter' to my mind placed him with Hudson.

Whatever place he finally finds as a novelist, his position as a writer on nature cannot even now be in question.

In these pages, others more competent than I have written about the *Chronicle*. I admit that I am not a great admirer of novels. Henry knew this and sometimes, as if to punish me, he used to come over and read his latest volume to me aloud. On one occasion, I retaliated by picking up the typescript of a play I had just completed, *Don Juan*, and made him hear every word of it. But in spite of my spite, we remained fast friends.

The only criticism I ever ventured to give him over the *Chronicle* derived from his failing of almost total recall. I told him that I counted my lack of memory as a literary advantage. I urged him to cut, delete and write with a pair of scissors. He did not take my advice or any offence. He was essentially a compulsive writer. This compulsion was derived from his loneliness and that was, of course, partially a cause of it. The *Liebestod* of Tristan was his theme: Henry searched but never found Isolde. And if he had, he would inevitably have driven her off. The paradox was, his nature was creative but self-destructive. He wrote eight hours a day and then rewrote. Even his postcards and letters carry the burden of marginalia and after-thoughts.

I do not know what place the *Chronicle of Ancient Sunlight* will find in English Literature. But I do know it cannot, nor will not (perhaps unhappily), be ignored. Those fleas seeking their PhDs are bound to alight on it. I will venture only these comments: that it attempts to do for the 1914-18 war what Tolstoi achieved in *War and Peace*. It does succeed in reliving (or redying) that era in a way that no Hugh Trevor-Roper can ever produce. If the book has a fault, it is, I think, because it is too autobiographical and detailed. As Eliot said somewhere: 'Art should be self-suppression, not self-expression.'

Of course Henry and I had our jokes and our squabbles. Only some of these, fortunately, come to my mind. I do remember when *The Times* asked me, some fifteen years ago, to write his obituary. I agreed to accept the commission, and asked Henry over for luncheon. To my surprise, he accepted with alacrity. 'Did not coming here interrupt your morning schedule?' I asked him. 'Not exactly,' he replied. 'You see, *The Times* have commissioned me to write your obituary, so I wanted to ask you a few dates.' Our laughter spilled our coffee.

The *Telegraph* printed an obituary. A nasty piece in which the writer, masked in anonymity, accused Henry of being a Nazi because in one of his novels the farmer makes a prisoner of war stand to attention in his presence when spoken to. I wrote to the newspaper and asked: 'Since when were an author's views to be identified with those expressed by the characters he had created? By that criterion Shakespeare could be accused of wishing to be King of Scotland, and I, after writing *Lucretia*, could be condemned as a rapist.' The letter was unpublished.

Certainly, Henry like very many writers had need of a hero. The dreamer seeks the man of action. Byron chose Napoleon; Pound had, I noticed, a photograph of Mussolini on his desk; Henry looked up to T. E. Lawrence, Mosley, and, even to Hitler. But had not Neville Chamberlain, the Duke of Windsor and others, many others, bent over backwards to placate the little Corporal, to do anything to avoid another European bloodbath? Before we deride Henry or castigate him for his political beliefs or sympathies, should we not ask what were Dante's? And whether his political enthusiasms are now considered relevant to his literary reputation?

It is the privilege of writers to be mistaken; great writers can be most mistaken. I cannot think of a single exception. This leaves me wondering in what particular area I most err. . .

One of Henry's most constant attachments was to my wife, Rose Marie. 'I think she is the most beautiful

woman I ever saw,' he told me. Their relationship remained wholly platonic, and thus endured. It was to her
he ran, with tears in his eyes, when his wife, Christine,
left him.

And soon after this, Henry heard that I was taking
Rose Marie and my daughter for a holiday. 'When are
you going?' he asked casually. I told him. 'Where?' 'Sicily
to start with; then on to Rome, Florence, and Venice.'
Without consulting me further, Henry went to my travel
agent in Barnstaple and arranged to book on the same
flight and in the same hotels.

He and I squabbled mildly a good deal on this journey.
I recall leaving a pizza uneaten in Florence because he
kept baiting me with his political notions which he knew I
didn't hold. Then, as we stood by the Grand Canal, by
the Rialto bridge, he remained deliberately unimpressed.
'It's a sort of sinking Ilfracombe,' he said of my favourite
city. His annoyance with me then was because Pound had
asked Rose Marie and me to luncheon and I had not
taken Henry too. I did not because I knew Ezra was
incommunicado. Indeed he never spoke a single word
to Rose Marie or me during the meal. And to bait me
further, when we visited the Uffizi Gallery in Florence
Henry had refused to come in to see the pictures, but had
sat in the hall reading the Sunday *Observer*. He was frequently capable of this kind of childish perversity, which
generally, as it did in this case, punished himself more
than others. Frequently, he would motor over for dinner,
then march up the hill again before the meal was served,
only to return later to beg for a hunk of cheese.

Henry consulted me about his idea of giving all his
manuscripts to Exeter University. Having sold most of
mine to Texas, I advised against it. But he was adamant
that his work should remain in Devonshire. I eventually
accompanied him to this ad hoc Presentation, to which
the Vice-Chancellor came late, then received the gift

without adequate acknowledgement or grace.

And like other contributors to this book, I was immensely saddened and angered when every tawdry Honours List omitted Henry's name.

But as Oscar Wilde wrote in relation to Swinburne: 'Only writers have the prerogative to honour writers.' So I will here give Williamson the Order of Merit.

'To buried merit raise the tardy bust.'

This author died, cornered by contemporary cant.

Ronald Duncan, 1978

PATRIOT'S PROGRESS
Ruth Tomalin

A MEMORY OF HENRY WILLIAMSON in a Hampstead café in 1967; with the striking looks of his later years, silver hair, dark sea-tan, brilliant hazel eyes becoming deep-set. He was talking very quietly about dieldrin and what it was doing to the peregrine falcons.

That was the summer of the Flower Children. The café was filled with the restless tinkling of little bells that — as someone wrote at the time — made all London sound like a Swiss valley. But gradually all other voices stopped, and not a bell stirred. Everyone was watching and listening to the stranger.

Henry Williamson always had this special rapport with the young, who have responded for fifty years to his writing as that chance audience responded to his personality. 'Flower power' would hardly have been in his line at any age; what they had in common was the urge to change the world by thought.

He was just nineteen when the Christmas truce of 1914 on the Western Front destroyed his faith in the men who were running the war.

Discussing the word *Freiheit* with some German soldiers, I learned, to my startled dismay and then happiness, that they believed they were fighting for the same causes and ideals as we were. It was a great mistake, that was clear to me: and if only the people in England could learn what I had learned . . . the War could not possibly continue.

(*The Children of Shallowford*, 1939)

1

Of course, no such miracle happened. Instead, a few days later, 'fraternization with the enemy' was forbidden by both sides. In the British Army, the penalty was death.

In 1918 the young veteran turned to hopes of the post-war world. While resting from the battle-front he began to write an ambitious thesis, *The Policy of Reconstruction*. Then came a second turning-point in his life; he picked up a copy of Richard Jefferies's visionary essay *The Story of My Heart*.

It was to me a revelation of total truth . . . my entire outlook changed. A life devoted more or less to pleasure, after my military duties, was ended. I had found, I believed, my purpose in life: to extend Jefferies's truth of redemption through Nature to my fellow men.

(*Some Nature Writers and Civilization*, 1959)

The thesis became a novel, the first of a tetralogy, *The Flax of Dream*, telling the story of 'Willie Maddison'. A sentence from Francis Thompson's essay on Shelley was to give the keynote of the first book, *The Beautiful Years*: 'So beset, the child fled into the tower of his own soul, and raised the drawbridge.'

But the books, as written, would not support a tragic theme or point a political moral. Love of Nature was too strong, and the urge to describe country scenes, remembered in brief escapes from his suburban home in Kent, or newly discovered in Devon. Even in the final book, *The Pathway*, where the young ex-soldier hopes in vain to found a new world order, what stays with the reader is not the tragic ending but the wild beauty of the Burrows and the gentle character of Mary Ogilvie.

'Ancient sunlight' seems an epithet better suited to these books than to the later *Chronicle*. Comedy kept breaking in; so that his father, reading *The Beautiful Years*, complained, 'He is lampooning his own people and his old school, and I refuse to read further.'

This was unfair — the lampoons were extremely lenient, the characters drawn with sympathy — but it was typical of their edgy father-son relationship. The book was just finished, and accepted by a publisher, when the new author reached his third turning-point: their decisive quarrel.

> In March 1921, through circumstances over which I had no control — the circumstances being my own feelings — I was abruptly homeless. 'Now, I warn you,' cried my father . . . 'that if I find you in this house again, I shall have no alternative but to summon you for trespass. You have made my life an intolerable burden for the past six months. Your writing is merely an excuse to loaf, and to lead an idle, worthless life . . .'
>
> (*The Sun in the Sands,* 1945)

But he was not really homeless; he knew where he was going.

At school, a bored and inattentive child, one sentence in a geography book had caught his interest: Exmoor, he remembered, was 'noted for red deer'. At eighteen, on a solitary holiday, he had discovered Exmoor for himself, 'a dreamy country, floating on sunshine', and had watched buzzards and pipits, fished for trout, and seen his first otter. Now he raced off to North Devon on his motor bike, rented a tiny cottage in Georgeham, grew a beard — that 'symbol of emancipation', Harold Monro said — and began the years of wandering, observing, and hard desk work that turned the gifted beginner into a great nature writer.

In the fresh exhilarating life he saw everything around him with intense feeling, and put down what he saw in truthful and musical prose; at first with a tribute echo of Jefferies.

> I have made a pool of stones where the swallows and martins can go for the mud to build their homes. Beautiful it is to see,

in the shadow of the trees, these birds alighting softly on a
boulder, or by the pool's edge, and shovelling the red mortar in
their beaks. They are timid restless things, rising into the air at
the least noise. I have passed many hours in watching them,
noting the number of times they came in a minute, and how
they mixed fragments of dried grass and straw with the mud . . .

(*The Lone Swallows*, 1922)

Such writing gives an impression of fluent ease; but all his
life Henry Williamson would correct and re-correct his
scripts, over and over, in differently coloured inks; often
revising the books yet again for new editions. *Tarka the
Otter*, he said, was 'recast and rewritten seventeen times'.
It was published in 1927, and a year later brought him
the Hawthornden Prize and fame.

By now he was married, with two small boys; and the
family removed to a thatched house in a river valley running down from Exmoor, an idyllic setting for the
country life he felt all children should have. A daughter
and two more sons were born here, to play in the deer-
park and the river; sometimes, in happy moods, joined by
their father.

I was one of them, I had got back, for a while, to the land of
enchantment, of unself-consciousness, to the world of otters,
deer, salmon, water, moonshine . . . the only world in which
perhaps there was consistency, form, integrity. Back again in
the house, with letters, bills, and typescripts, the ever-pressing
need to turn feelings into words, this world too often faded,
and the children were problems of noise, dirt and even irri-
tation; but never of resentment.

(*The Children of Shallowford*)

Meanwhile he was spending thousands of hours watching
the 'clear water stream', to produce a second masterpiece, *Salar the Salmon*. On the surface at least the
success story continued. But that of course was not the
whole story.

Once, knowing how he had suffered in childhood from family criticism, I asked him: 'Surely, after *Tarka* and *Salar*, your father must have been proud of you?' His reply: 'Do you remember what D. H. Lawrence's father said, when his first book was accepted?' (And who could forget that classic reaction: 'Fifty pounds! An' tha's niver done a day's hard work in thy life.') But now he had begun to see the past with new eyes. After the age of thirty, he said, he found the very traits which he had once hated in his father, developing in himself.

These traits he described frankly in *The Gold Falcon*, a novel showing the disillusionment of another war survivor, 'Manfred'. Written after a first visit to America, its New York scenes are some of the liveliest he ever wrote; but subjective bitterness predominated, and the book was chiefly a blend of harsh self-critical facts and reckless fantasies. Published in 1933 — anonymously at first — it underlined the cost, in nervous stress, of a dozen years' ceaseless dedicated writing.

At the age of thirty-two Manfred had all that a man could desire, so his friends believed — genius; a beautiful and tender wife; two fine children; an Elizabethan house standing in a valley, with a garden of old-world flowers and fruit trees; a trout stream; a fast car for visits to London . . . At thirty-three Manfred was sick of all things, while knowing that the sickness was not of all things, but of his own inactivity . . .

(*The Gold Falcon*, 1933)

Two books about Devon village life in the nineteen twenties had an 'underlying theme of regeneration'. Now, in search of a new and active life, he turned to practical regeneration; buying a holding of two hundred and forty near-derelict acres on the Norfolk coast — ominously known as 'the Bad Lands' — and setting out to make it into a top-grade farm. He began with every kind of handicap — lacking capital, knowledge, experience, and with no suitable house for his family. And again, through sheer hard work and determination, he succeeded; though the record often makes painful reading.

But again this was not the whole story.

Over the second half of his life hangs the question, often asked by friends as well as critics: Why didn't he stick to his country writing? Why involve himself in politics?

The answer is, or should be, that his conscience would not let him alone. He was still haunted by Christmas Day 1914, the slaughter that followed, and the broken promises of the post-war world. To do nothing would be a betrayal.

The 'land fit for heroes' was becoming so in Germany: in Britain, some men of thirty had never worked since leaving school. No jobs for them. Many slum children ate only every other day. Few had seen a plateful of cooked food.

(*Lucifer Before Sunrise*, 1967)

Hence, in March 1936, the words in his foreword to the one-volume edition of *Flax*: 'I salute the great man across the Rhine, whose life symbol is the happy child.'

Hindsight gives this a ring of sheer folly. But many people just then were trying to see the best in Hitler and his régime, in the hope that war could be averted. Harold Nicolson—with no such illusions—had written in his diary: '23rd March 1936. The feeling in the House of Commons is terribly "pro-German", which means afraid of war.'*

Henry Williamson had learned that Hitler's regiment was one of those with whom he and his comrades had mingled in friendship on Christmas Day 1914. Persistently and wistfully, he saw the German leader as a fellow-soldier who knew the truth about war and would never

---

* Harold Nicolson, *Diaries and Letters: 1930-1939* (London, Collins, 1966).

start another; while the new Germany, to him, meant workers' battalions, building new roads — as, in his own sphere, he was doing on 'the Bad Lands' — and children properly fed: in contrast to the slum families of Britain, whose condition was soon to come as a shock to the more fortunate who would take them in as evacuees.

Sir Oswald Mosley's party, he thought, with its plans for the expansion of British farming, offered a similar spirit of hope to a decayed countryside. His own farm had been undertaken as part of the idea of 'a new resurgent Britain'.

After the outbreak of war he reproached himself — 'Oh, why didn't I fly to Germany, to beg him not to march into Poland? I was a coward not to go' — and clung to the belief that Hitler did not want to destroy Britain.

During the Fifth Column alarm after Dunkirk he was arrested under Section 18B of the Defence Regulations, and suffered a moment of despair as he left home under guard.

The garden which he had not yet been able to begin to tidy up was still a tangle of nettles and buttercups and old bicycle frames and wheels and heaps of broken glass and crockery, deposited over the hedge . . . This was the real England: not Birkin's (Mosley's): not his own little books, or Ralph Hodgson's *Song of Honour*, or Shelley's poems, or Wilfred Owen's, or the prose of Richard Jefferies, or the music of Delius. The real England was based on the deflowered Thames below the Pool of London.

(*A Solitary War*, 1966)

He was briefly imprisoned, then released to carry on his 'solitary war'; but the farm as a family base did not survive. In October 1945, 'a farm which in eight years had been raised from a state of near-dereliction to an official classification A', was sold.

He went back alone to Devon, to the hut he had built

long ago, with the *Tarka* prize money, in a high field below Exmoor. In 1949 he remarried; and, while watching another small boy grow up, he devoted himself to a task which he had been planning for half a lifetime. This was *A Chronicle of Ancient Sunlight*, a novel in fifteen volumes, recreating his whole life with the aim of showing it as a microcosm of history.

This lone voyage around his own world lasted twenty years; and at the end his achievement was not acclaimed, nor did he receive the honours given to others in old age. But again he had kept faith with himself. He remembered, too, how Hardy, Bennett, and Galsworthy had praised his work in the old days, when the revered T. E. Lawrence was also his friend.

Twenty years before the first word of the *Chronicle* was written, he had told Edward Garnett of this project; and was urged not to go back to 1893, but to 'plunge straight into 1914'. Excellent advice, perhaps, if he could have taken it; for the series took on a new stature with the 1914 book *How Dear Is Life*, and this high level of interest was sustained throughout the five books covering the first war. Had he allowed these five to stand alone, reserving the rest of his story for straight autobiography, the critical interest they aroused might have given them their true status as a great war classic. From his readers, that quiet 'underground army', such recognition has never been in doubt. One has only to watch the library shelves to see how continuously the whole *Chronicle* is read, together with the reprinted country stories and *The Flax of Dream*.

But, if not always the best judge of his own work, when he came to help others he could be as clear-sighted as Edward Garnett, and as generous. In the later nineteen forties, with a friend, he edited a little review, *The Adelphi*; giving a start to some of the generation who, like his own, had gone from school to war, and now wanted to write. He published their apprentice work, and often made time to write letters as friendly as those he had received in the early Georgeham days from Walter de la Mare and others; remembering what this had meant to the solitary beginner.

In the icy winter of 1963 he sent £50 to a writer in a London garret, 'to help you keep fed and warmed. Mind you spend it. Don't worry about repayment.' Another was helped to obtain a travelling award. That was typical; and he could be equally thoughtful to strangers. On summer evenings, playing his beloved *Tristan* or Delius records in his house in Ilfracombe, he would open the front door as well as the windows, so that strolling holiday-makers could share his pleasure.

Tous nos malheurs viennent de ne pouvoir être seul. Perhaps he was always a natural solitary. Yet he was also a compulsive letter-writer — the envelopes, in his lighter moods, ringed about with his owl motif — an amusing talker and splendid reader aloud. The later novels were criticized as lacking good dialogue; but this never applied to the country stories. For the old Devon speech especially he had a deep affection and a faultless ear; and those characters, with their gentle or gritty idiom — 'They'm a lot of bliddy rogues, noomye!' — were never so vivid as when he read the tales himself.

A gifted broadcaster, in his late seventies he also wrote and appeared in a memorable television film, *The Vanishing Hedgerows*: though describing himself with disgust as 'an amateur who can yap volubly off the cuff, but a damned bad actor who FLUFFS and panics . . .'

'Amateur' was a highly emotive word. The years on the farm, and wartime labour troubles, had sharpened its edge for him; but his standards had always been high, in practical as well as professional matters. Gear and tackle must be perfectly kept, firewood stacks laid down like wine — 'nothing burned under three years, and the heavy timber matured to seven years'—cars, tractors and fishing-rods expertly handled. In this he was like his father; and he would recall with compunction how, as a boy, he had borrowed and sometimes spoilt his father's things.

Self-deprecation was never far away. When his first wife, 'Gipsy', wrote to him, 'You are a wonderful old boy', he quoted this with pride; but added bitterly, '*I know what I am.*'

Some early hopes were realized before he died. Fish were returning to the Thames: this had been a cherished dream. High farming had long since restored the fields of East Anglia; now ecologists had to urge that some weeds and wilderness be left for 'nettle-creeper' and butterfly. Young people had happy faces, not prematurely old, like the London poor of his boyhood.

In his last years, done with writing, he liked to go every day to Exmoor, where Jefferies once walked; and to stride off alone into the sunlight of the Chains, adopted as his own country sixty years before, when he came there first as a dreaming boy with a long journey ahead.

HENRY

Kerstin Hegarty

I FIRST MET HENRY WILLIAMSON through some great friends with whom I was staying in Devon, near Henry's home. I remember I had not been well, and was struck by Henry's concern—I think that was one of his greatest qualities, his immense kindness. He was a marvellous friend, loyal and sympathetic; and I noticed that he never leaped to hasty conclusions about people or situations, but always tried to see everybody's point of view. I think you could define it as seeing the *whole* of things. In Henry's series of novels *A Chronicle of Ancient Sunlight* Phillip Maddison, the hero, is an example of this attitude: he tries to understand both sides in the two World Wars.

Henry understood animals, and the story of his dog Robbie shows the care he would take in a difficult situation. This dog was an 'innocent', as Henry put it; like Henry, he did not want to kill anything in Henry's field, but preferred to live and let live. Robbie became friendly with a wild hare; they used to chase each other and play together. Eventually Robbie became old and incurably ill. To quote Henry himself: 'For one whole morning I stood near him in my hilltop field, and when he had dug hard at a mousehole, and his snout was well down and Robbie was blowing down it, wuff—as though to drive the fieldmouse into the open—his eyes closed against the dust, I fired. He never saw me, he never knew he was hit, he lay quietly on his side, as though to sleep.'

Robbie appears in Henry's final novel, *The Gale of the*

World, as Bodger, cross between foxhound mother and terrier father, who is trained to find his master should he (Phillip Maddison)—described by Henry as his doppelgänger—go blind. For Phillip, like Henry, was blinded by mustard gas in the 1914-'18 war; but recovered his sight later.

I went to work for Henry for a while in Ilfracombe—secretary, cook, housekeeper—for me an immensely valuable and rewarding experience. Working in the hut or studio in the field at Ox's Cross was always fascinating. Henry would read his manuscripts to me before I typed them out, and I shall never forget sitting by the log fire drinking delicious beverages to keep out the cold, feeling that body and soul were being equally well nourished. Henry was a communicating reader, and always interesting; verse and prose became immensely alive when read by him, and he often read from the works of other writers too. Francis Thompson, Richard Jefferies, John Donne, T. E. Lawrence, to name but a few of his favourites; and I learned a great deal from listening to him.

He was also a vivid public speaker. I heard him twice: once after a Wild Fowl Dinner, and later in Devon, when he gave a talk on living in a Devon village. In his many television appearances also he came across very well, as himself.

I remember our many walks along the cliffs and moors, particularly around Baggy Head and across the Burrows behind the coast of North Devon. The countryside and skies were opened up to me as never before. I suppose I am not especially observant, but I improved; birds, insects, and the life of nature in general became a marvellous entity. These walks became exciting experiences, not just a way of getting exercise. Often we talked, and Henry had a seemingly inexhaustible supply of amusing stories and quotations; of these I remember in particular one from Keats which seemed singularly ap-

Ox's Cross, Georgeham (close to Henry Williamson's Field)

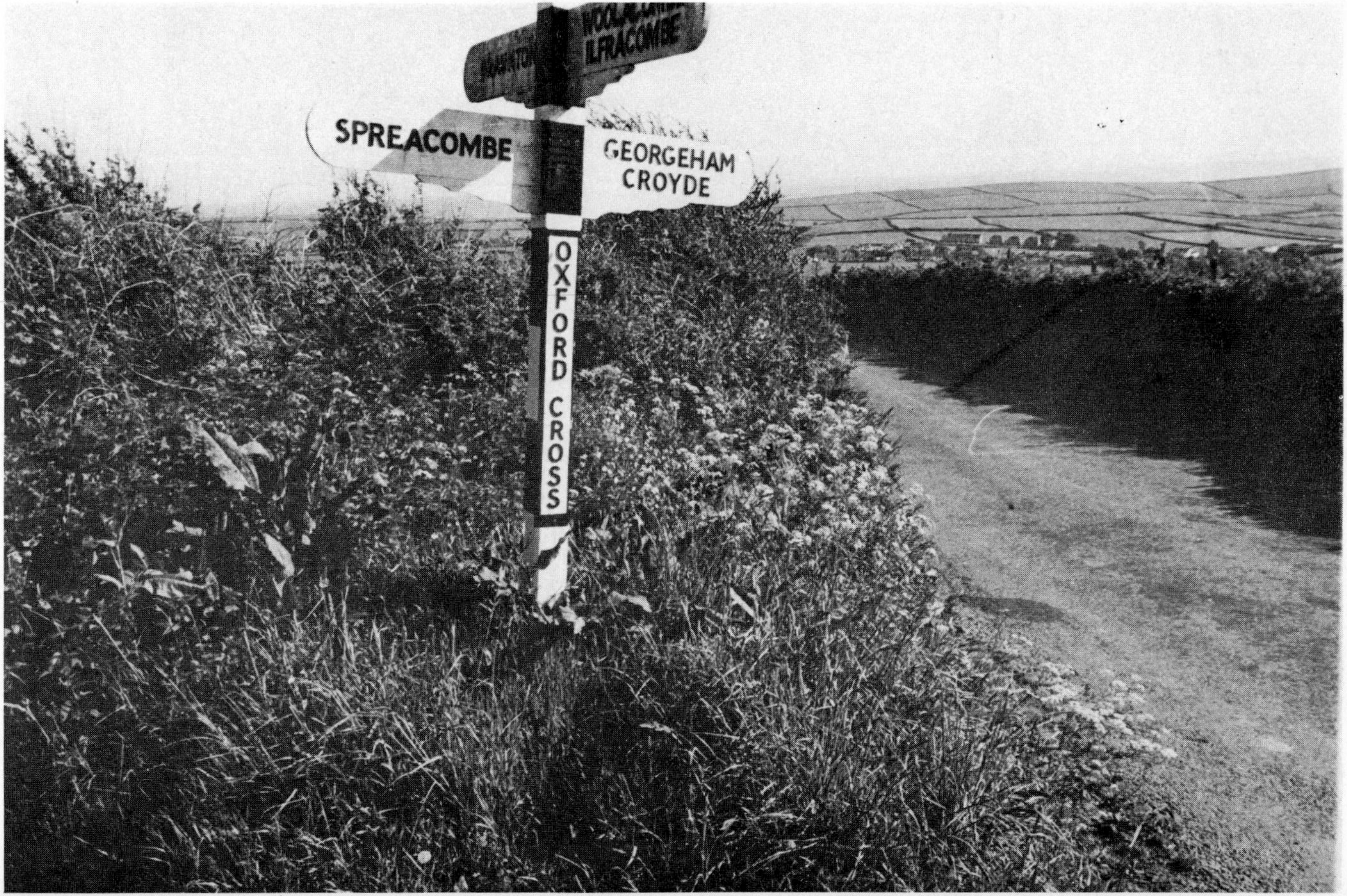
ILFRACOMBE
SPREACOMBE
GEORGEHAM
CROYDE
OXFORD CROSS

propriate as we gazed down at the restless sea beating
against the rocky Devon coast:

> The moving waters at their priestlike task
> Of pure ablution round earth's human shores.

Henry was an amusing, lively companion, always the life
and soul of any party. He had a truly wonderful sense of
humour and of the ridiculous. When the day's work was
over we often went to pubs, or to the cinema, to while
away the winter evenings when we did not go to see
friends. Sometimes Henry read to me from what he was
writing at the time; he seemed to need reassurance for his
work, and I hope I gave him some. Like any true genius
he had difficult and moody moments. How could such an
intensely creative writer *not* have some depressions and
doubts about his work? I think these were the varying
moods of a truly sensitive person. At such times he needed
someone to listen and reassure him; or else he needed to
be quite alone.

One day when I was there he said he needed solitude;
and that he wanted to climb up to the heights of Dartmoor to a spot where five rivers have their separate
sources in the peat near Cranmere pool. To revisit where,
nearly two thousand feet above sea level, the Taw and
Torridge begin their lives. He mentioned before he went
that he might be away for perhaps three weeks; so I
hurried out to buy some provisions, thinking that it was
hardly the weather for long walks, but that it was probably best to let him go if he wanted to. Among the food I
bought was an exceptionally large piece of cheese — it
weighed six pounds — and Henry duly disappeared, along
with the cheese, at two o'clock in the morning.

The evening before, a violent storm had broken loose.
Force Nine gale; the whole West Country was lashed by
sea and wind. I cannot remember how it happened, but

Henry at Home. (Ox's Cross, 1950's)

the next day I locked myself out of the house, and found myself in the freezing cold, wondering how on earth Henry was faring on his walk. Finally I borrowed a neighbour's ladder and climbed in through a window; which was hardly an auspicious beginning to three weeks alone!

Once inside the house again I turned on the electric fire and started to type out some fascinating letters from T. E. Lawrence which Henry wanted me to copy. After a while I thought I must find something to warm myself with. I hunted around and found some red wine. Delicious! The more I typed, the more interesting the letters became, and the more I drank. For it was so cold. The storm raged outside, and I felt very much alone. I remember eventually sitting completely bemused, staring at Henry's First World War riding boots standing at the foot of the stairs, and being completely convinced that they were on the march.

The next day Henry returned; soaked to the skin, but a new man. He had walked by compass and map across Dartmoor, despite the fact that all the little brooks were raging torrents, and that on the high ground a Force Nine gale was whipping up water into an icy mist. He brought back untasted that dreadful block of cheese. We could not get rid of it. Somehow it never seemed to diminish, and when we tried giving it away nobody was interested. In the end it was eaten by screaming seagulls.

After I had returned to London from Devon I used to type articles for Henry from time to time, and we saw each other often; lunches, dinners, theatres, and always Henry was the same fascinating friend. You could never be bored with him, he had such a young attitude to life. That is why, I think, he got on so well with young people; he was still so young himself. Sometimes I saw him at Ronald Duncan's home, where we had first met. There were many interesting discussions, but Henry still made

everybody laugh; and on the beach he larked about with
seaweed like a three-year-old. That reminds me of one
morning when I came down to the kitchen in Ilfracombe
and found my housekeeping and recipe notes covered
with completely unrepeatable jokes. I still have these, and
they often make me laugh. Henry came to my wedding
party, and I heard from friends afterwards that he was
last seen leapfrogging down the street in the company of a
crowd of young people.

In 1964 I went with Henry and a press photographer to
France. It was the fiftieth anniversary of World War I.
Henry had been commissioned to write a series of articles
for the London *Evening Standard*, and we were going to
revisit all the 1914-'18 battlefields.

This was a strangely moving experience — one that is
difficult to convey in words. The atmosphere of that
sombre sad part of France and Flanders, although so
orderly and peaceful now, was still blood-soaked. The
articles were called 'Return to Hell'; and that it must have
been for Henry. We first went to Vimy Ridge, and in the
final paragraph of his first article he wrote: 'Now, after
nearly fifty years, I find myself upon these ancient battlefields to report on — what? In me there lives the ghost of
my young self, compassionate, estranged, accepting all
things with clarity.'

We went to the German graveyard, 'The Labyrinth'.
A terrible place, where chalk once covered the graves, so
that nothing could grow for a long while. Acres and acres
of black crosses: a very different place from the beautifully kept British and French cemeteries. Henry felt that
the tall black crosses had been put there by the French
government as a warning — almost a condemnation — and
that it showed the inability of the French Establishment
to forgive.

We went first to the Somme; then up to Ypres, to the
old battlefields which are now well farmed arable and

pasture—or else cemeteries. It was difficult to believe
that these places had once been upheaved and totally
desolate battlefields. We stayed at little hotels—I remember one place where they were very suspicious—and
Henry told them that he was a 'vieux soldat'; they still
looked rather hostile until it was established that we were
English. Then they relaxed and became very friendly.
Anti-German feeling still ran high. Ypres is strange, it is
so completely rebuilt and resurrected; yet I remember
waking up there in my hotel room with a terrible fear.

For me the most moving place was 'Plugstreet Wood'.
A beautiful quiet new wood now, once again a covert for
game. In the middle of what seems a haven of nature lies
a small British cemetery: gentle, very rural, and not too
immaculate. It was tender, young, wild. Sadly, so much
youth had perished there. Henry was there, a teenage
soldier, in 1914.

I quote from one of his *Evening Standard* articles.

How quiet it is. A nightingale is singing. 'Summer, summer,
summer, the soundless footfall in the grass.' Gossamers drift.
Faraway in the depths of the wood a dove is moaning—boo-
boo-roo-roo—over and over again, with pauses. Strange how
wild pigeons have changed since I was a boy in the woods of
Kent. Now they nest in August; then it was March. Due to
change in the farming pattern?

Dappled shadows fall on these quiet headstones within the
mason'd walls. These oaks must be eighty years old at least.
How did they survive that frightful bombardment in April
1918, during the Germans' last drive for the Channel Ports?

Henri Barbusse, in his classic *Le Feu*, wrote that when you
hear that a comrade has been killed it is like a blow . . . 'Only
later do you begin to mourn.' These names . . . killed 19th
December 1914 . . . again and again . . . This stone roots one
to holy ground. Holy? Are you not sentimentalising the past?
No: I am remembering my comrades.

Look at this one, please.

5500
R. Barnett
The Rifle Brigade
19th December 1914. Age 15.

Below is carved the Star of David, and that he was of Stoke Newington, London.

The eyes drop their tribute salt.

In later years I saw Henry less often. I had two small children, and lived some distance away. His letters still give me immense pleasure — they interest, entertain, fascinate and reassure me — and above all keep Henry alive for me. For me his friendship is one of the greatest and most rewarding experiences of my life.

HENRY WILLIAMSON

Alexandra Burgess

I

HOW DID I COME to know Henry Williamson? How does anyone come to know and understand a writer? The answer is — from the pages of a book. It began, at the age of fourteen, when I was ill in bed and was presented with a pile of books from the County Library, one of which was Williamson's *The Starborn*. I believe that this book is, for the perceptive, the best introduction to H. W.'s work. Who is the Starborn? What is his message? These are questions that ring echoingly from beginning to end of this small masterpiece. Each character is created with skill and delicacy, so that it is impossible to doubt the existence of Ung, the doll, the Quill Spirit, and the many other spirits that live so tangibly in the trees and water, and in the light of day and night. At a first reading *The Starborn* might seem to be just a fantasy or fairy story about a baby taken from its mother and returning to earth many earth-years later. But as with most of Williamson's work, there is a message here: a very clear and sincere message of the Kristos — a theme that is the foundation of the great series of the novels of Henry Williamson.

After *The Starborn* other works were read: and then *The Pathway* was discovered. A discovery which was for me, as it has been and will continue to be for others, a turning point in life. There was something in the atmosphere of this book that told of a man who was not only a great writer but one who had gone through many ordeals,

experienced much loneliness, misunderstanding, and unhappiness. There was nothing to say that the hero, Willie
Maddison, was anything but a creation of the author's;
nor was there anything to contradict the wild assumption
that the creator himself was, or had been, torn with
anguish at the blindness and stupidity of the post-war
world. There was nothing—yet there was everything.

With reflection, curiosity became compulsion, and the
whole range of Henry Williamson's work was chosen for
further study. I formed the bold resolve to write a 'thesis'
on Williamson and his work. A difficult task, which in
the end it proved impossible to achieve as it should have
been achieved. A letter, seeking advice and guidance,
was sent to Mr Williamson himself—one of many such
letters that every writer of eminence receives from time to
time. I doubted if any reply would be received; but when
an answer came, the address caught my eye. I knew from
his autobiographical writings that his home had been in
Devonshire; but since reading *The Story of a Norfolk
Farm* I had believed him still to be living in the Eastern
Counties. It was with great joy that I saw that his present
home was not more than four or five miles from Woolacombe, in Devonshire, where I was planning a four weeks'
working vacation.

On arriving in Woolacombe inquiries were made con-
cerning the 'Hermit of Ox's Cross'[1]; but little was learned
except that Mr Williamson had once owned a very noisy
Norton motor-bike (a fact which I already knew from
many incidents recorded in his writings). A tentative
letter was composed, and posted. Would Mr. Williamson
grant me the five minutes' interview requested? I was
terrified lest he should think me just another autograph
hunter. But in reply came an invitation to call on him.

This invitation filled me with delight and fear, excitement and apprehension, and a desire to forget the whole
mission although it meant so much to me.

At last, on Sunday, three o'clock arrived, and after completing the washing-up I left the hotel. The sea was grey; the wet sands looked cold and uninviting. 'Up the mountain road' had been the instruction in the letter, so I started to climb the steep hill to my goal, some four miles away. Each side of the road was flanked with green hedgerows; the fine but quickly falling rain enhanced the brilliant colours of the flowers, ferns and leaves so closely entwined. The fresh smell of the damp earth mingled with the salty sea-breeze from over the white-flecked waves: a breeze that grew stronger as my steps took me higher. Several times I had to pause to rest aching calf-muscles or to allow touring cars to pass in the narrow lane. Down below, the line dividing sea and sky was undetectable — only the white foam of the breakers as they crashed upon the lonely beach gave any sign of movement in the still picture: a picture that gradually grew smaller as my steps took me onwards.

I must have walked for an hour before reaching the dead and dying trees[2] which I knew stood guard near the black palisade gate leading to the field — the field that had filled my thoughts for so many days.

The time was only ten minutes past four, and although I was expected at any time between then and the half hour my nerves were in such a condition that I thought it better to try and calm down before pushing open the black gate. I bided my time by leaning over a gate opposite, while for some minutes I studied several cows that plodded and snorted through mounds of mud-caked grass. Footsteps along the lane broke through my thoughts, and I turned in time to see a tall, grey-haired gentleman with a staff pass by, accompanied by a small child who also carried a stick. With a shock I realised that this was the man I had come to see — or so I thought, for the only photograph I had seen had shown a soft, clean-shaven face, whereas my fleeting glance had seen a brown weather-beaten face with a moustache. But something told me that the tall striding figure was Henry Williamson.

In a state of panic, I was far too agitated to call or run after the man and boy as I watched them pass down the hill. With a new fear clutching me I crossed the road, pushed open the black gate, and ran down the path. I stopped short as I came to the edge of the field. On my right was a white hut, but as it seemed to be deserted I went on and soon sighted another building and, to its left, a caravan. Something about the sight reminded me of far away places and memories. The whiteness of the walls and the soft smoke from the chimney of the second hut made me think of a scene in Switzerland: a small wooden cabin at the top of Mount Rigi, where time no longer existed, and only the soft tinkling of the cowbells far below, and the occasional rising of the cloud-mist, revealing snow-covered sun-kissed peaks, were reminders of the world that waited far below . . . Here I had the same feeling—that strange timeless immortal feeling that only breaks through to one's mind in a dream . . . But here one stood only a few moments' walk from a comparatively busy lane, and only a few hundred feet above civilisation.

In spite of the smoke curling so deliciously from the chimney of the hut, I decided to go first to the caravan. There was no need to knock; the door was opened by Mrs Williamson. 'Miss Wigginton? Henry and my little boy have just gone to meet you.' My heart sank at these dreaded words, as I explained my foolish terror. Mrs Williamson laughed, and said that she understood, and that her husband would understand too, being himself a very shy person. I was immediately at ease, and could even smile as I saw her pick up a police whistle, which, she assured me, would soon bring them hurrying back. Unfortunately, my terror reappeared as I saw the two figures returning, and thought how like Moses was the tall, grey-haired figure that was approaching.

My thoughts then became more and more obscure, and in my memory this first meeting with Henry Williamson has about it a dreamlike quality. During the time I was with him (my 'five minutes' turned out to be a period of six hours) I vainly struggled to take in 'facts' for the sake of my work—my main reason for seeing him—but was immediately conscious of a strange sympathy towards him.

During tea I felt that I was floundering hopelessly (especially after upsetting the hot-water jug!); and my knowledge of this writer's keen insight into human nature and character made me feel like a drowning man in a whirlpool. He was tired—so very tired. A fatigue caused by working into the early hours of the morning. I was told not to worry if things did not go well. 'So many young people think it is their fault if conversation lacks and tempers are frayed,' he said; 'but do not put it down to any failings of yours—I am exhausted.'

Conversation went on. He asked me about my work, and hearing that I was interested in subnormal children he wryly remarked that I must be practising on a subnormal author! Questions were asked and answered on both sides—time passed slowly, and I began to think that the interview, although as informal as could be, was a failure; and then suddenly I sensed that the atmosphere had changed. Nothing special was said; the rain still fell, the fire still flickered, the eight-year-old child still sat at my side, and his father continued to smoke a cigarette, facing me across the narrow table.

I had no idea of the hour, but I thought it must be time for me to thank my hosts and go back through the mist-filled lanes to the hotel. But I did not want to go. I was now seeing things in a different perspective. The scene had changed from a series of two-dimensional sketches to a picture that held me by its unity, warmth of colour, and its unique subject. A few minutes later I was asked, and not as a matter of convention, 'You are staying to dinner, aren't you?', and almost before my delighted mumble of a reply could make itself heard I found myself shelling freshly-picked peas.

That afternoon, Mr Williamson told me, he had written an article on his schooldays.[3] Would I like to hear it? He quickly disappeared outside into the greyness of the evening, and crossed to the studio — the hut with the smoking chimney near the gate. His wife looked up, and smiled understandingly. 'It's rather a lot to take in all at once,' she remarked, 'but it will all sort itself out.'

The article, when read aloud by its writer, conjured up visions of a very small naughty boy continually being 'walloped', in scenes reminiscent of those in *Dandelion Days* and *Young Phillip Maddison*, stories, in the *Flax of Dream* and *Chronicle of Ancient Sunlight* series, of the youth of two cousins.

Somehow the conversation turned to war, which the young Henry Williamson had experienced during the long years of 1914-1918, and which he had reported 'factually' in *The Wet Flanders Plain* and *The Patriot's Progress*: a theme on which he had meditated long and deeply. Picking up his novel *The Golden Virgin*, he began to read. For the first time in my life I was overwhelmed by the beauty and vividness of the spoken word. As the scenes of battle, with all their horrors, passed before me I realised, again for the first time, how much an author is part of his writing. H. W. was no longer with us on that cold, wet evening, but lay once more in the trenches, surrounded by the dead and wounded — hearing the cries of the tormented sufferers. Later I asked him how far he projected himself into his main characters. 'Practically all the time,' was his reply. 'That's what some people object to.'

After dinner Williamson resumed his reading. I sat transfixed, unable to take my eyes from the figure whose words recreated and relived these scenes of the past. The gentle voice read on and on until the past was the present and the present was one with the past. I found it hard to believe that the quiet, rather abrupt, shy man I had met that afternoon was the animated person who now faced me — alive with the fire of creation.

Darkness had descended, and now it was time to go. On the way back I thought of everything that had happened and had been said during that afternoon and evening. Of death Williamson had remarked, 'I am not frightened; it will come. I think about it but do not worry. What does worry me is that so much appears to prevent one finding space wherein to write, to rest, and to meditate.' And when I asked if he was fond of music he answered shortly, 'Of course. I live by it.' The mental picture of him which I had built up from his writings had in some respects been confirmed, in others shattered. In *The Story of a Norfolk Farm* he had prophesied that 'in time students will find delight in finding out about the author from the pages'. How true. From his books I had imagined a personality whose chief qualities had been quietness, kindness, and patience. As to physical appearance, I had had no preconceived ideas. I had hardly thought of him as anything other than a nature writer whose disposition would be extremely gentle and whose eyes would reflect his inner tranquillity and sincerity. But now I could see what he meant when he wrote that 'Some young people reading my books had wanted to meet the author, thinking that some of the effects of the reading would be shining about his personality' (*Story of a Norfolk Farm*).

His personality shone — but not from any inner tranquillity or peace of mind, though I believe that such may be hidden deep below the exteriorly-observed tensions of a writer or artist of nervous temperament, to well up and shine out in his work. As with some of the great contemplatives—St Augustine, for instance—who can hardly have been easy to live with.

He had talked of war, of the many depressions by which man's soul is tortured; he had spoken of peace and love, of music and people: but whatever the subject, I was chiefly aware of one thing: an inner power . . . strength of mind, the power of the spirit. Even the gentle smile he bestowed on his child who lay with his head on his lap whilst he read was charged with a hidden force.

I had proved my theory; but in its proving I had found more than I had ever expected or imagined. The light that pervaded the world on that rainy day in August was the light that shines through *The Flax of Dream*; a series completed before I was born; and dealing with events in the life of his doppelgänger (as he puts it) William Maddison, who was drowned in the estuary seen from the hilltop, in September 1923. Of that estuary, of those characters, the solitaries and the sensitives of three generations have dreamed—and come from many places to walk over the Williamson country. The man I met last year was a man whose voice had come to me from a world which existed fifty, sixty, seventy years ago. This voice, which told of weakness and strength, storm-fury and gentleness, revealed not only contrasts but harmonious blending comparable with the tones and shades of the Nature that was his true home, whose beauty, harmony, and freedom he strove to preserve.

3 August, 1958

II

ON THE MORNING of 13 August 1977 our car slid slowly to silence with several hundred other vehicles trying to enter or leave the road to Bodmin. It was hot: windows were wide open, the baby snoozed in his chair beside his six-year-old sister, husband's fingers drummed impatiently, and the radio pumped out love and lust in differing tones and tempos.

Music tones faded. 11 a.m. news. 'The man who wrote *Tarka the Otter* and *Salar the Salmon*, died today. Henry Williamson, in his 81st year . . .'

Pain struck hard between the ribs, breath failed to come. The shock was indescribable. I knew that my dear old friend had been ill in a nursing home for some time, so I should have anticipated this news; but nothing could have prepared me for the despair and complete disbelief that engulfed me that August morning.

This state of non-acceptance lasted for several weeks; books and letters spanning years of a unique relationship only irritated the situation. How could H. W. be dead? How could so much vitality, physical and nervous complexity that I had first encountered, as a nervous student so many years ago, now cease to function? Death had touched me on several occasions, but only as a shadow: not this total eclipse.

We were unable to attend the funeral; so on Monday 31 October I said goodbye to my husband and children for three days. With an overnight case in one hand and a copy of *The Pathway* in the other I boarded the train for Devon. Thetford, Ely, Liverpool Street to Paddington, all negotiated successfully; but with a certain amount of anxiety, as it was eight years since I had last been on a train journey. It was only when safely en route to Barnstaple that I was able to relax and revel in the pages of *The Pathway*. How marvellous to walk again with Willie and Mary along the Burrows, wondering at her gentleness and her deep understanding of her sensitive 'boy'.

At Exeter another change: onto the local train, to find myself practically the sole occupant. Now I was really in

Williamson country, as so many thought of it; among them James Farrar in 1944, when he wrote: 'On a good day the undulating skyline of the North Devon coast is obvious (Exmoor etc.). I hope to fly over to have a look at the Williamson country.'[4] The sun played tag with the clouds as the train followed the river's course; to my delight three herons were sighted, standing sentinel, too superior to be ruffled by our passing. I have always loved these majestic birds, although many countrymen and fishermen are irritated by their presence. Kenneth Allsop observed, in his book *In the Country*: 'How many of my speckled beauties [trout] have gone into that scrawny craw. It puts a strain upon my alleged love for birds to embrace this uninvited visitor, bearing its long dagger of horn, elegant though it is in a leggy, lean Vogue model way.'

Barnstaple at last. Out onto the platform, suddenly wondering where the night was to be spent. This problem was quickly solved after counsel with the ticket collector, and within minutes I was settled.

Now to take stock. The journey had passed speedily; several times I had found myself bubbling with excitement, but was this because, for the first time in six years of motherhood, I was experiencing my freedom? Or was I in delusion, retracing steps into the past, refusing still to accept the truth?

The next morning, Tuesday, was grey and blustery. I had consulted the bus timetable the previous evening, so after visiting a florist I decided to go first to Ilfracombe, before travelling on to Georgeham. The weather grew worse; rain rattled on the windows of the bus, and the greyness of the dripping passengers emphasized the dearth of life in a holiday centre out of season as we descended the hill into 'Combe. Familiar steps from the bus station, round the corner, and up a steep incline to the small row of cottages near the harbour.

I had first visited Henry's cottage in 1958, before it had become his main home. It was in the middle of a terrace; the front door led into a small hall; to its left was a room which ten years later was to become my work room. Upstairs there were two bedrooms; downstairs the kitchen and a study where the delicious smell of beechwood always lingered. On that first occasion Henry had raced up and down the stairs of the empty house, alight with enthusiasm, and had lit a fire of paper and sticks in one of the rooms. Magic!

Early in March 1968 I started to work for Henry in a secretarial/Girl Friday position. At nine o'clock each morning I would pick up the milk, turn the handle of the door, and call 'Good morning, Henry!' Sometimes he would come bounding up, or down, the stairs with an answering 'Good morning, Alex!'; on other days a 'Hello' would come from somewhere in the cottage; sometimes there would be only a grunt, or nothing at all. It was from my reception in those first few minutes that I learned if his work had been satisfactory since the previous day. His post would occupy him, and then I would prepare his breakfast, which he would usually eat in the kitchen, enthusing over or berating the correspondence he had received. Breakfast time could be traumatic. He adored bacon and mushroom and bacon and egg, but insisted that no fat be added to the pan, that the egg or mushroom be fried in the dripping from the bacon. Unfortunately, the bacon did not always exude any dripping, or not enough, and consequently the pan often stuck. I solved this problem by smuggling in a small lump of dripping each morning, but was terrified that he would discover this deception. His mood would always lighten after he had eaten — 'boiler restoked, ready to go'; but like Phillip Maddison in the *Sunlight* novels he failed to eat regularly.

At this time he was working on *The Gale of the World*, the final volume of *A Chronicle of Ancient Sunlight*.

After clearing the table I would go up to my room off the hall, answer any general correspondence, retype changes in the mss, and alter my copy correspondingly. There were many rewrites of particular scenes; time and again he would remanipulate the characters and their words until both of us were screaming with confusion. It seemed impossible for him to put down his pen and say 'It is good,' and accept it. His worry was feverishly intense, and he was for ever trying to make perfect what was already perfect. One episode stands out vividly. We had toiled for over a week on a scene where Miranda is alone with Peregrine, her father. At last it was right; he was satisfied, and apparently serene. At 9.30 p.m. he arrived at our house, with the manuscript, utterly distraught. He had reread the chapter — it was wrong! wrong!

This constant passion for perfection haunted everything he did, and was indeed the ruination of many of his personal relationships. In his 'fictional' autobiography *The Sun in the Sands* he wrote: 'Often I imagined that somewhere under the sky was my companion, my sun-maiden, who would share with me all the loveliness of my new world . . . for in the glitter of water was the spirit that one day I would find, one day, one day, one day.' I believe his search for the perfect companion remained with him until the end of his life.

Although *The Gale of the World* took up most of the time I worked with him at the cottage, he also became involved in the creation of a television documentary for BBC 2, directed by Patrick Garland. His nervousness was acute, and he needed constant reassurance before the filming dates; but once he was in the midst of the 'action' he relaxed and enjoyed himself tremendously. Similarly when he was approached by Roy Plomley for 'Desert Island Discs' on Radio 4. Unfortunately I was in Germany when these programmes were transmitted, and missed them both.

After the last of the *Chronicle* manuscripts had been delivered to the publishers we made several attempts at working on *The Scandaroon*, a delightful story of a pigeon (happily published in 1972); but at that particular time his enthusiasm was not great enough to allow him to become fully absorbed. His life's work was nearly completed, and he felt empty and anxious — as a mother feels lost when her child has left home.

As I stood gazing at the empty cottage now, memories showered round me like the rain. Gone were the net curtains I'd bought for the front room, the inlaid table at which I'd worked, and the moulded fruit arrangement under its glass cover. I wanted to open the door, call 'Good morning, Henry,' and run downstairs to the study; to share again the music of Tristan and Isolde, Parsifal, The Shepherd's Song, Delius; to listen to Henry's gentle voice, far, far back in time, telling of his experiences; to march with pepper pot against salt on the table across the Somme, and to laugh at the human antics of Bodger of Great Snoring, or the inimitable Globe-Mornington.[5]

Referring to the content of Henry Williamson's writing, Colin Wilson said that it was like having a best friend who is enchanting and exasperating by turns.[6] This applies equally well to Williamson's character. There were times when he was an extremely difficult man to work for; but he was also compelling, delightful, great fun, with a wicked sense of humour, and invariably kind and generous.

Would his immediate neighbours remember me? It had been a long time; but my knock brought welcome, warmth, and tea. We talked for an hour; then farewells, and return to the bus station. On a fine day the road from Braunton to Georgeham is exquisite; through Croyde village, past the sands and up the hill overlooking Saunton, and down into Georgeham. On this day the Gods from Valhalla screamed their furies across the Burrows, and tore the sea to frenzy; violence personified, with no sign of abating.

I wandered up to the Field, passing the church on my left, approaching the 'dead and dying trees' from the opposite direction to that which I had taken on August 3, 1958. The water was gushing down the hill in rivulets, carrying the last of the leaves. The gate was open: a great yellow house confronted me; only a dog answered my call.

The wooden hut where T. E. Lawrence had slept ('He was sunlight'): did the black kettle occasionally sing on the open fire? Did Sally the spider or her descendants still live by the hearth? Were the tools in order on the bench?

The Studio: candle-light, books, wine, fascinating scrapbooks of cards and curios — logs stacked neatly against the outer wall.

The Caravan. Walking in unexpectedly after our return from Malta in 1967. 'Alex! how marvellous! let's have some tea.' Clonk of kettle, the twinkle of 'Pass the sugar, booger!' No recriminations for having been a poor correspondent, just the loving laughter of two friends re-united on a summer's afternoon.

That day had been the beginning of a three year residence in the West Country, living in Westward Ho!, Ilfracombe, and Braunton successively. Henry was a frequent visitor to our house before and after I became his 'sounding board'. We walked and talked through the seasons, along deserted winter sands, over the Burrows and moorlands; we chatted happily to summer visitors, followed the course of the rivers at Lynmouth, whose flooding he depicted in *The Gale of the World*, and watched the surefooted goats as they startled birds from the gorse in the Valley of the Rocks.

I remembered the fearful anticipation experienced on my first visit to this field nineteen years previously. That emotion was now replaced by a heavy sadness still too deep to comprehend. I took one last look, then retraced my steps down the hill to the churchyard.

The Norman church, overlooking Skirr cottage where he had first lived when he came to Devon, had been a part of H. W.'s life for many years, and now he lay in the shadow of its tower. The grave, as yet unmarked, was bordered by a hedge swollen with foliage and glistering berries weeping black tears from the rain. I pushed my umbrella into the grass, and crouching beneath it I spread over the muddy earth the flowers I had been clutching all day.

The rain cried with me.

*   *   *   *

Henry Williamson was a complex, controversial character whose life's work will continue to be a source of debate. Some acclaim his nature writings and ignore the later novels; others do the reverse. From this one man we have gained insight into the wondrous excitement of our rapidly diminishing natural world; a brilliant, sensitive, and accurate account of a vital period of twentieth century history, and imaginative penetration into the lives and minds of characters in whose portrayal so many of us have felt the shock of self-recognition. I hope this complete picture of an era will one day be acknowledged and applauded.

A thanksgiving service for Henry Williamson was held in London at St. Martin-in-the-Fields church on 1 December 1977, which would have been his eighty-second birthday. For me the service was memorable not only for the perceptive and sincere tribute given by the poet Ted Hughes, but also for the diverse people who attended. I wondered that one man could have reached out and touched the differing lives of so many of his fellow creatures.

The impression Henry Williamson made upon my existence was absolute since he was undoubtedly the greatest influence in my life. I mourn his passing, but derive comfort from the knowledge that I can walk again, as in the early years, with the spirits of the trees, with Willie, with Phillip and his myriad dreams. His words will embrace eternity.

20 June 1978

NOTES

1. Title of an article on Henry Williamson by Maurice Wiggin, in the *Sunday Times*.
2. Henry Williamson replanted his beech clumps with oak and beech about this time.
3. Henry Williamson, 'Out of the Prisoning Tower,' in the series 'John Bull's Schooldays': *The Spectator*, 22 August 1958.
4. James Farrar, *The Unreturning Spring*.
5. Bodger of Great Snoring: Phillip Maddison's dog in *The Gale of the World*. Globe-Mornington: night-porter at the Barbarian Club in *The Gale of the World*.
6. Colin Wilson, 'Henry Williamson', in *The Aylesford Review*, vol. iv, no. 4, Autumn 1961.

A TRIBUTE TO
HENRY WILLIAMSON

Diana Mosley

HENRY WILLIAMSON was a good and much-valued friend to us, intensely loyal to my husband. In any interview he gave to the newspapers, or on the wireless, or for television, he seldom let an opportunity pass to praise Mosley's political beliefs and ideas and his opposition to the second world war. He did this, not only of late years now that it has become respectable, but at a time when it was very unpopular to hold such views, and when moral courage was needed.

The first war, in which Henry fought as a young man, marked him as surely as if he had sustained some terrible wound; it crippled him, and he suffered from it; but (as the German proverb says), what does not destroy, strengthens. The shy, almost diffident man Henry always remained had a hidden strength within which gave him rare courage.

Everyone of any sensitivity who fought in France in the first war suffered intensely from the experience, and Henry was hyper-sensitive. It was only after the second war that he could bring himself to write about the first in his immensely long novel *A Chronicle of Ancient Sunlight*. Other writers were more fortunate. The poet Robert Graves, for example, got the first war out of his system and off his back with *Goodbye To All That*, a brilliant book which influenced the new generation too young to have seen the war at first hand.

While Graves was unburdening himself in this way Henry Williamson, who was not yet ready to write about the theme which really interested him, was writing his nature books. Books about animals are always best sellers in England, from *Peter Rabbit* to *Watership Down*. Only the other day a list of the most-read books of school-children was headed by *Black Beauty*. In *The Story of a Red Deer*, by John W. Fortescue, the author manages to combine two English obsessions: while rabbits and stoats talk like Walter Gabriel in 'The Archers', the red deer, noble creatures, have got Oxford accents. In all these books the animals talk, and in some they even wear clothes. It is by no means only children who read them.

'Escaping' from his memories of the horrors of war, his first nature book, *Tarka the Otter*, won the Hawthorn-den Prize for Henry Williamson; and he could have made his fortune, as well as being one of England's best-loved writers, if he had continued to direct his sharp and penetrating gaze upon fish, flesh, and fowl for the rest of his days. Though nothing irritated him more than being 'typed' as a nature writer, because of the excellence of *Tarka*, and of *Salar the Salmon*, this was his fate. Publishers begged him for more, but they had to make do with the Chronicle.

Henry saw the murderous second war coming with deep despair. Could nothing be done to stop it? He gave Mosley unwavering support in his campaign for peace. In the late nineteen-forties Henry, driving a fast sports car, sometimes visited us at a house we had in Wiltshire. Appalled by the spectacle of shattered Europe, and by England's diminished power and influence, he wondered aloud whether there might not have been something more he personally could have done to stop the second war.

The moment was approaching when the first war and its traumas were far enough away for him to be able to write about them. The subject absorbed him and filled his whole being. After the second war the novels of his

Chronicle succeeded each other every year or two. I remember reviewing one of them in *The European*. I had found the book hard going, and I suggested that the 'hero' (who was Henry himself, but with none of Henry's originality, cleverness and charm) might perhaps have been made more attractive, so that the reader would feel more involved in his fate. He was, or seemed to me to be, so colourless that interest in his doings flagged. (Probably Henry's point was that the novel should be about Everyman at war, not about an exceptional man, a poet.) This review of mine was answered by a letter to *The European* from Richard Aldington, himself the author of a notable war novel, *Death of a Hero*. Aldington said that Henry Williamson's descriptions of the life of a soldier at the front were absolutely accurate in every particular. Such an opinion is valuable. Henry was so truthful that his immense saga will always be read so long as there is anyone who wants to know exactly what it was like to be in the front line in the first world war. This was what he wanted to do, and what, as Aldington says, he succeeded in doing.

SOME MEMORIES OF H. W.

Brocard Sewell

IN SEPTEMBER 1957 the editor of *The Aylesford Review*, a literary and theological quarterly published by the Carmelite Order, invited Henry Williamson to contribute to a forthcoming issue of the magazine which was to contain articles on Williamson and his writings. In his reply, dated 15 September, he said: 'I think I could do an article as you wish: on the theme, which underlies my work now, that God is love is honour is duty and self-sacrifice: and lovelessness is the lack of those invisible and spiritual motivations of life. In my new novel I hoped people would see that war, massed lovelessness, was of less importance to the individual than the search for that which man must have if he is not to perish.' In the late autumn the Henry Williamson number of *The Aylesford Review* appeared,[1] with articles by William Gore Allen, Malcolm Elwin, and John Middleton Murry, together with Williamson's 'Some Notes on *The Flax of Dream* and *A Chronicle of Ancient Sunlight*'. At that time the *Review* was being printed at St. Albert's Press, the private press of the Carmelite Fathers at Aylesford; but in 1959 the press was moved to Llandeilo, in Carmarthenshire, where the Order then had a house of studies. That summer Henry paid a short visit to the Carmelites at Llandeilo, and while he was staying there he read to them one evening his lecture on *Some Nature Writers and Civilization*,[2] which earlier in the year he had given, as the Wedmore Memorial Lecture, to the Royal Society of Literature. The audience on that occasion had been deeply moved by the speaker's concluding words. I find them no less moving today as I read them in the quiet of my friar's cell, and recall the lecturer's gentle voice. They seem to express the essence of Henry's faith in the possibility of a better life for men and women after the horrors and sufferings of two world wars.

I write these words after our North Devon Festival week, and particularly a night spent among boys and girls listening to and living joyfully in the rhythms of Humphrey Lyttelton's band in the Queen's Hall at Barnstaple. There was a shimmer of life in the hall; hundreds of happy faces below the platform, eagerly watching, happily listening, gently swaying; and there was tenderness too, among the young people, as pony-tailed heads were stroked within protecting arms of teen-age boys. I thought of linnets among the gorse in bloom upon the Sussex downs, almost dreamily uttering their gentle notes in the south wind; I thought, too, that one of the alternative titles for Lawrence's *Lady Chatterley's Lover* was *Tenderness*. And it seemed to me with my own memories of such poverty seen among less fortunate people in my boyhood and early youth — of young children with almost old faces prematurely set to endure misery — the faces which Jefferies had seen in the slums of Swindon — it seemed to me that now the age of so-called 'idleness', or leisure to relax, was a possibility: and that possibility was in part due to two wars after which, despite all, the slums had begun to die. And that the 'near-madness' of the fully articulate of one age can sometimes be sanity and clear-sightedness to the next.

But we must not condemn those who do not perceive so quickly as the visionaries, for it is only a question of time; and in the words of Richard Jefferies, 'Now is eternity; now is the immortal life.'

Williamson became a generous contributor to *The Aylesford Review*, for which he wrote articles and book reviews, always refusing payment. A number of letters from him appeared in the magazine's correspondence columns. Some of these contributions were signed simply

Henry and Sarah Williamson. Aylesford Priory, c.1961

with the initials H. W.; one book review, a full length
article, appeared over the pseudonym 'Green Jacket'.[3]
The reason for the pseudonym will be clear to anyone
who reads the article. *The Aylesford Review's* circulation
never exceeded five hundred copies, and was usually
below that figure. By 1960 it was in financial difficulties
because of a heavy increase in printing costs. To help it,
Henry generously offered to allow St. Albert's Press to
print and publish in a limited edition a chapter from his
unpublished autobiographical writings. The result was a
small book, *In the Woods*, which was issued in an edition
of one thousand numbered copies, of which fifty were
printed on special paper and signed by the author. All
profits from the book's sale went to *The Aylesford
Review*, the author forgoing royalties. This was typical of
Henry's generosity. (The episode recorded in *In the
Woods* will be found treated in fictionalized form in his
novel *Lucifer Before Sunrise*.)

In 1961 the magazine was again being published from
Aylesford. Henry then became a frequent visitor to the
priory, where he met a number of the younger *Aylesford
Review* writers and artists, who often spent weekends at
the priory guesthouse. Henry fitted into this group like a
kind of elder brother. It included Frances Horovitz,
actress and poet; Jane Percival, a painter from the Royal
College of Art; Nicola Wood, an RCA-trained textiles
designer; Michael Hastings, playwright and novelist;
Michael Horovitz, poet and translator; Oswald Jones,
photographer; and Penelope Shuttle, who had just published her first novel, *An Excuseable Vengeance*. A little
later Henry introduced to the group Ann Quin, whose
first novel *Berg*, had been causing something of a sensation. Henry had recognized her talent, though it was
quite alien to his own. In a letter of May 1964 he says:
'*Berg* I regard as an innocent allegory or moral tale
sprung from an impulse similar to that which impelled

In the Library, Aylesford Priory, 1960's

Hardy's phrase, "If way to the better there be, it exacts a
full look at the worst." . . . At the end of this morality
play, decorated by the familiar and nowadays fairly innocent four-letter words (as indeed used now and again in
private living), it all begins over again: the characters are
as they were. Grace has not yet come . . . Superficially,
Berg is a sordid story. But it more than repays study.
Beneath the "illusion" of its reality one perceives a talent
of rarity and grace.'

These weekends among his friends at Aylesford were
happy times for Henry. In July 1963 he sent this message,
on a postcard from Cefalù, in Sicily:

I did enjoy my visit to Aylesford last Sunday, among the
friends.

Here, too, a holy building is being restored,[4] part of the
modern European renaissance. Building, building, everywhere, from Palermo to the Costa Brava. The Aylesford
Review is part of that renaissance — the widening of life can
only widen, & clarify, the essential Truth, which is conveyed by
poetic images, symbols, and creative work. Lux fiat.

Many thanks,
Henry

Soon after Henry's death a writer in the correspondence
columns of a Sunday newspaper said that Henry was
jealous of younger writers, and never helped them; and
that he never acknowledged the help that he received
himself when a young and struggling writer. This writer
showed little knowledge either of Henry Williamson or his
writings. Henry was not without human faults and failings; he could be touchy; sometimes over quite imaginary, or certainly unintended, slights. A number of his
friendships ended sadly because of this over-sensitivity.
But to the young he was invariably helpful and encourag-
ing, often in very practical ways. If he saw talent, he was
quick to advance it. In the late 1940s, when he was edit-

ing *The Adelphi*, which he had taken over from Middleton Murry, he published work by a number of unknown, or as yet little known, writers: among them Charles Causley, James Farrar, and Ruth Tomalin. In 1960 he helped to find a publisher for the war letters of Lance-Corporal Robson,[5] who was killed in North Africa in 1945. In his introduction to this book he said that he believed that *Letters from a Soldier* would take its place among the very best of the hundreds of war books that he had on his shelves. He was no less generous to his own contemporaries, and never tired of affirming the excellence of two novels of the first world war: Wilfred Ewart's *Way of Revelation* and Victor Yeates's *Winged Victory*. In Williamson's autobiographical writings there are many grateful references to the men who helped and encouraged him when he was young: Edward Garnett, Arnold Bennett, John Galsworthy, J. D. Beresford, Beverley Baxter—who published his early nature articles in the *Daily Express*—and Constant Huntington (of Putnam's).

In June 1964 *The Aylesford Review* held a literary conference at Spode House, the Dominican retreat house and conference centre in the grounds of Hawkesyard Priory, in Staffordshire. About fifty people came, and Henry spoke on Richard Jefferies and W. H. Hudson. Other speakers were Colin Wilson, Laura Del Rivo (a young writer who had just published an elegantly written first novel, *The Furnished Room*), and Alan Neame, a fellow-contributor with Henry to *The European*,[6] who spoke on problems of biblical translation. This was a very successful weekend, not least from a social point of view. In a postscript to a letter written on June 20 Henry said: "I *loved* Spode visit. It was a jolly fine party, the best literary one I've ever attended.' This was the first of a series of such Whitsuntide meetings at Spode House, and Henry came to a number of them.

In May 1965 he presented to the University of Exeter a large selection of the manuscripts of his books and other writings. The question of the ultimate destination of these manuscripts had been worrying him for some time. They were of considerable value, and could have been sold for a very large sum to the Humanities Research Centre at Austin, Texas, or to some other American university foundation. In the end he decided to give them to Exeter University, so as to keep them in the county where they had been written, which was the setting for many of his tales and novels. The presentation took place on the afternoon of Friday May 14 in the lecture hall of the university's Washington Singer Laboratories. At the beginning, a slightly incongruous note, which Henry seemed to enjoy, was struck by the late arrival of the Vice-Chancellor, who said, after apologising for the delay, that as a man of science he was not well versed in literary matters, and did not know a great deal about Henry Williamson. There followed three twenty-minute talks on Henry Williamson and his work,[7] and then came the formal presentation of the manuscripts, and their acceptance by the Vice-Chancellor on behalf of the University. After the presentation the guests attended a sherry party given by the Vice-Chancellor in honour of the occasion. It was a crowded affair, for in addition to Henry's family and friends, and members of the University, there was present a large contingent of members of the West Country Writers' Association, who were in Exeter for their annual reunion. Originally Henry had expected about 150 people, but in the event there were nearer three hundred. In the evening he gave a dinner party at the Royal Clarence Hotel for his family, friends, and some senior members of the University, in all about sixty people.

At Whitsun 1968 Henry attended a conference on 'The Restoration' at Spode House. A lecture by Mr. Donald

Bruce on Thomas Shadwell, the 'Orange Laureate', was followed by a reading of Shadwell's comedy *The Sullen Lovers*. Henry had been offered any part that he might care to take. Modestly, he chose the minor rôle of A Country Gentleman ('A Grave ill-bred Coxcombe, that never speaks without a Proverb').

1969 was the year of publication of *The Gale of the World*, the fifteenth and last novel in Henry's *Chronicle of Ancient Sunlight*, and it had been decided that this event should be celebrated at Spode House in some appropriate way. On the last evening of the conference, which had heard papers on the life and work of Pope Felix V, Frederick William Rolfe, Father Ignatius of Llanthony, and Eric Gill, Mr Dennis McWilliams spoke on 'The Works of Henry Williamson', after which there followed a short recorded talk on Williamson by one of his former secretaries, Kerstin Hegarty, who was unable to be present herself. Mr Trevor Hold then read his poem 'Ancient Sunlight'.

ANCIENT SUNLIGHT

for Henry Williamson

(NOTE: the hay which was used to build up the funeral effigy of Henry VII after his death in 1509 was analysed a few years ago and found to contain, besides straw, the dried remains of common vetch, hairy tare, lesser knapweed, selfheal, broad-leaved dock, buttercup, cow parsnip and three types of grass.)

> Through the glass of Time, discoloured with
> The dust of centuries, the sun still shines,
> Preserved within this dead king's effigy.
> Its fire has gone: it is no longer bright
> But parchment-ochre, cracked with age,
> Yet it illuminates, like specks in its shaft,
> Fields as beautiful with their flowers and grasses
> Thrusting upwards to the ancient sunlight
> In all the eagerness of that year's spring,
> As those in which I walk today.

Finally, at about 10 p.m., Henry was presented with a cake bearing fifteen lighted candles, and his health was drunk with acclamation.

Lecturing in front of Henry Williamson could be an ordeal. He was not good at concealing boredom, and sometimes he could not resist the temptation to enliven the proceedings for those sitting near him — he rarely sat near the front — with humorous *sotto voce* comments. Or, pen in hand, he would compose ribald verses, with farcical illustrations, which made it very difficult for those sitting near him to contain their amusement. He had a kind of friendly mocking humour that was peculiarly his own. In 1966 *The Aylesford Review* published a special Aubrey Beardsley number, to coincide with the Aubrey Beardsley Exhibition at the Victoria and Albert Museum. There were two articles on the exhibition, one on Beardsley and the *Savoy* magazine, and one on 'The 1890s and after in France'. There were several illustrations, from drawings by Aubrey Beardsley. Henry sent this comment, on a postcard dated 14 October:

An excellent number, the Autumn Review. Aubrey Beardsley by Robert Booth most interesting, and 'full of meat'. And dear Jane Percival's Notes on the Exhibition follows, to complement it. What a love that girl is. And a new writer, hitherto unknown to me, 'Brock' Sewell, the well-known badger-digger (an actor, I'm told, the original 'Man in Black' at Tinsley's Old Music Hall in 1889, father of Marie Lloyd), is a good new art critic. The drawings by Osgood J. Jones are really wonderful *pastiche, exactly* reproducing the period of the decadent nineties. But we want to know more about the Savoy Hotel. Mr. McClellan's article takes away the taste nicely.

The last conference that Henry attended at Spode House was in May 1970. He always enjoyed these occasions, and his presence was looked forward to and much appreciated. On the Sunday afternoon he would usually take

three or four friends with him and drive over to Cannock
Chase for an hour or two's walk. His companions on these
excursions benefited from his keen observation and
minute knowledge of the countryside and all its plants,
birds, insects, and animals. After three years' absence, he
had hoped to come again in 1974, for the celebration of
G. K. Chesterton's centenary, and in 1975, to speak on
Francis Thompson. But when the time came, he was unable to be there. He had always seemed immune from the
restrictions of age, but quite suddenly they caught up
with him. Long journeys by road or rail were no longer
possible; they had become too tiring. As early as 1972 he
seems to have sensed that his life was drawing to a close.
In a letter written in May of that year he said:

. . . I think of Belloc — and of Chesterton — with both of whom
I had an acquaintance, in the grand days of my youth — being
recognised, and accepted, is a serious and delightful and awe-
ful thing in youth. Can this they praise, be *me*? Verily, the con-
sort of God's genes in a man can make him feel small, and
humble . . . and aware of the truth of Creation — indeed, one
would dare to say, of the Creator — . It is the eve of June, and I
sit here in a summer eve of yellow, and muse; because the evening is quiet, light. And I feel I must write to you . . . Those
lovely times at Aylesford — and at Spode — and there was magic
there — a glimpse of the Magic — and then we must go, and
enter a penumbral shade, if not a little darkness: for once
again, after the immortal moments, we are but creatures leaving behind us a memory of the soul of a gathering of men and
women made gentle under the kindly eyes of those who had
seen God . . .

Enough of me. Sincerely I grieve, in the twilit room, for
absent and lost friends, some in death's dateless night — the
Pragger-Wagger has just passed over, HRH the Prince of
Wales.[8] He was such a dear boy, and man. I heard from a
connexion of mine, Sir Frank Colyer, who was a jaw specialist,
and attended George V. This is my only connexion with
Royalty; but not the only connexion with Loyalty . . .

Loyalty was one of Henry's most conspicuous virtues. It is eminently a soldier's virtue, and Henry was an old soldier. Loyalty is always to be admired, even if it is felt to be misplaced. Those who voted to deny to Henry Williamson the academic recognition that should have been his ought to have remembered that. In a letter of September 1974 Henry said: 'I know my own peers — Masefield O.M. who said to me "You have written more classics than any man alive." Galsworthy O.M. concurred.' The man who had been honoured with such praise was not much disturbed by the impercipience of Academe.

Henry was often depressed, but usually the source of depression was near-exhaustion. Perfectionist that he was, the writing of each new book was a kind of agonizing battle, that often had to be fought through several times. *Tarka the Otter* was rewritten no less than seventeen times. *The Gale of the World*, his last major book, was almost completely rewritten after it had reached the galley-proof stage. And after that, the first three hundred printed and bound copies were pulped, so as to allow of further corrections and revisions. Henry was fortunate indeed in the publishers, Macdonald and Co. Ltd, who backed the *Chronicle of Ancient Sunlight* when other firms had not the courage. He would often speak with admiring affection of Eric Harvey, the managing director of Purnell's, Macdonald's controlling company: 'A grand chap, a superb organiser of that £15 million group starting with £50 sergeant's gratuity (his father) at Taunton in 1919.'

His constant journeys to and from Bristol and London, for BBC radio and television programmes and other affairs, family problems, worries over the filming of *Tarka*, and numerous other demands on his time and energies, added to Henry's growing fatigue. At home, the hard work that he put in at the Field, keeping everything tidy, and tending his vegetable garden and small orchard, kept him fit; but the ever-pressing burden of his correspondence and his business affairs, on top of the strain of constant writing and rewriting, was another matter. In a letter of March 1969 he wrote: 'So here one is back at paper paper paper—letters, letters . . . I am over-worked and have 2000 letters unanswered . . .[9] The Chronicle is finished. It has left one empty and ALONE. And devastated. I am 73 and weary.' These moods would pass; and he was always happy among friends.

Henry was sustained in his life's work, against all failures, disappointments, mistakes, and misunderstand-ings, by his faith: faith that one day men would live peaceably together, 'under the fostering hand of the Creator', seeing clearly, in Richard Jefferies's 'ancient sunlight', that all are God's children and must live together in harmony. His novels were written to help us to see how wrong thought distorts the whole of human life, and sets us at variance with each other. Change thought and you change the world. Christ saw all things clearly, and we must learn from him to do the same. Henry's belief was more intuitive than dogmatic. He was not a great churchgoer. But he had a deep attachment to and respect for his own church, the Church of England. This can be seen in some of his Devon tales, and in his early novel *The Pathway*, in which the hero, the ex-officer Willie Maddison, gives vent to blistering denunciations of the hypocrisy of church-people, but is on good terms with the vicar, Mr Garside, who is sympathetically portrayed.

An intriguing figure in *A Chronicle of Ancient Sun-light* is Father Aloysius, an ex-Army chaplain who belongs to an order of 'Laurentian' friars, of which he appears to be the only member. He is an admirable man, and seems to be modelled in part on a chaplain (possibly more than one chaplain) whom Henry had encountered in the first war. Could he have met in the trenches Father Benedict Williamson, who had refounded the extinct male branch of the Brigittine Order, but remained himself the only member since he never succeeded in keeping any of the novices who came to him? In an essay on 'Reality in War Literature'[10] Henry praises *'Happy Days' in France and Flanders*, the war memoirs of Benedict Williamson, whom he describes as 'a popular and beloved padre'. This sounds rather as if these two Williamsons, who as far as I know were not related to each other, had met.

In a long article which he contributed to *The Aylesford Review* in 1969[11] Mr George D. Painter said that 'The basic truth of the Church has rarely been expressed more beautifully, or more acceptably to those who remain outside the Church, than by the words of Father Aloysius, in *The Golden Virgin*, to Lieutenant Maddison discovered wounded on the Somme: "the Virgin and the Child is not a symbol of what should be, but of what *is*, Phillip".' In a letter of May 1959 Henry said that he intended to ask the BBC if he could give a radio talk on 'Father Aloysius'; but nothing seems to have come of this.

Williamson had many Catholic friends. Probably the closest of them was the historian and satirist Dominic Bevan Wyndham Lewis. Another was J. B. Morton, Wyndham Lewis's successor as 'Beachcomber' in the *Daily Express*. Henry's admiration for the poet Francis Thompson is well known. As a young man, in the early 1920s, Henry paid some visits to the Meynell family, at Greatham, in Sussex; he was proud to have known Wilfrid Meynell, who 'discovered' Francis Thompson when he was a down-and-out on the Thames Embankment, and was the first to publish his poems. In *A Chronicle of Ancient Sunlight* Phillip Maddison's mother, Hetty, uses Catholic prayers in moments of stress, and has a devotion to the Blessed Virgin. She is not a Roman Catholic, but has learned these things at her convent school in Belgium. Some of Henry's letters of

1968, written at the time of the 'Humanae Vitae' crisis in the Roman Church, contain references to the Pope (Paul VI) which show a marked respect for his person and office, and an understanding of the difficulties of his position. In the monastic ambience of the Carmelite and Dominican priories at Aylesford and Hawkesyard Henry was always at home.

Henry Williamson is buried at Ham St. George (Georgeham) in a grave close to the hedge a few yards to the west of the church tower. In his book of tales *Life in a Devon Village* he has described the consecration of the new burial ground in Georgeham, an event which ended the five-year-old controversy recorded in *Tales of a Devon Village*. This new cemetery was consecrated by the then Bishop of Crediton. I would like to end these memories of Henry Williamson by quoting from his account of the Bishop's address, as the words seem to express so well his own simple belief.

The Bishop, who bore the name of Trefusis, was preparing to speak.

'We are come together with one heart and soul to dedicate this ground to God: for we are giving it to God this day. You are called to present to God what has been provided after many difficulties and trials. There are always difficulties in this mortal world, my children: nevertheless, while you are here on earth you must always remember that you have duties to perform to your neighbours. No man can live for himself only, and be a happy man; for man is so made that he attains serenity and strength by working with and for others.'

The Bishop spoke in a throaty voice, for he was very old; but there was sweetness in his face and gestures. His words fell slowly in the wan sunlight among the trees.

'I, who am old, and soon to die, have seen the graves of those I have buried pass away in time, forgotten or lost, until nothing is left but grass, and a lessening mound. Such is God's intention for all living things: to be, to bloom, to mingle in earth and air, in the hope and faith of resurrection in radiance beyond the hills of our mortal mornings gray. All of us have the journey down into darkness, even as the lonely hero of all, the Man among men, our blessed Jesus, whom we call the Christ.'

So the wise and gentle words ceased, and the white head was bowed in prayer; and in the moment of silence following, while our thoughts prayed for us, we were glad that we had listened.

NOTES

1. *The Aylesford Review*, vol. ii, no. 2, Winter 1957-'58.
2. Printed in *Essays by Divers Hands* (Proceedings of the Royal Society of Literature), vol. xxx, 1960.
3. 'Lucifer or Eosphoros', in *The Aylesford Review*, vol. ix, no. 1, Autumn 1967.
4. In 1963 the restoration of the medieval buildings at Aylesford Priory was still in progress.
5. *Letters from a Soldier* by Walter Robson, with an introduction by Henry Williamson: Faber and Faber, 1960.
6. *The European*, a review of politics, literature, and the arts, edited by Diana Mosley.
7. The talks were given by Ted Hughes, E. W. Martin, and Brocard Sewell.
8. The Prince of Wales: later HM King Edward VIII.
9. It *seemed* to Williamson like two thousand letters (about the same number that he received every year); but the actual number was much less.
10. In *The Linhay on the Downs*: Faber and Faber, 1934.
11. George D. Painter, 'The Two Maddisons' (review of *Love and the Loveless* by Henry Williamson), in *The Aylesford Review*, vol, ii, no. 6, Spring 1959.

A FREQUENCY OF PHOENIXES: SOME NOTES ON THE NATURE-WRITINGS

Sylvia Bruce

> Could we employ the ocean as a lens, and force truth from the sky, even then I think there would be much more beyond.
> *The Story of My Heart*[1]

> Let us get out of these indoor narrow modern days, whose twelve hours somehow have become shortened, into the sunlight and the pure wind. A something that the ancients called divine can be found and felt there still.
> *The Amateur Poacher*[2]

IF, with birds' eggs snug in their nests before us, we see only a dizzy array of damned dots, we would be too close, and ill-informed, to tell a Seurat from a Sisley, let alone intrusive cuckoo from innocent hedge-sparrow or sedate tree-pipit. So with the work of Henry Williamson: when it looks to us a welter of what might be charlock and what could be couch-grass, of neglected, desolate fields, Bad Lands clogged and claggy, rugged beyond conquering, it may be that we are misusing the lens or treading too closely upon the artist's heels—and that we have not done the preparatory work, as readers, of learning a difficult new vocabulary and clearing from our own minds those rampant prejudices that proliferate like sprouting weeds.

To read him is, in the strictest sense, a harrowing ex-

perience. It is to be crushed, broken up, or pulverized as
with a heavy frame of timber or iron, the purpose of
whose iron teeth or tines is to cut the clods and stir the
soil. The soil will have already been subjected to dis-
ruption by a plough that, to prepare ungrateful ground
for receiving seed, shares with sublime indifference the
bodies of worms, or parts the nests of fragile, quivering
birds the labourer would rather rescue.

'Nature-writings' is an artificial category, since Nature
is everywhere, often animate, and Man a substantial part
of it. I may, perhaps, be forgiven, therefore, if instead of
addressing myself immediately to the *Collected Nature
Stories*, for instance (some of which might more properly
be regarded as tales of the supernatural), and singling out
therein all depictions of non-human animal life, I discuss
some recurrent themes, imagery, and problems, of the
opus as a whole.

In the collection of youthful writings, dedicated to
Richard Jefferies, called *The Lone Swallows*, the essay
entitled 'Boy', which begins as a startling and poignant
sketch of a lad employed as a crowstarver or human
scarecrow, develops into an elegy for a whole vanished
world, comparable to Housman's 'land of lost content';
for wherever may be the carrion and the hooded crow,
the reckless tattered boy, like so many of his contemporaries and those of Henry Williamson, did not survive
the Great War:

Once the illusion of boyhood arose out of the wheat and the
trees and the birds in the sky: a living thing, brilliant as the sun
up through the hornbeam leaves. Other eyes may be finding it
there now; my little boy may see it when he is older; but for me it
is lost for ever, though sometimes a smell of burning wood or a
forlorn far cry may bring a glimpse in the mind. For between
that vision of green wheat and singing larks and sunshine lies an
immense darkness and corruption, a vast negation of all beauty,
as of life broken and moving backwards to the original void.[3]

Yet the sun that sears is the sun that quickens: '. . . Still
the beautiful clouds lie over the downs, the larks are singing, the wheat rising green. There is hope in the wide and
open sky.'[4] The essence of the entirety of Henry Williamson's work is alchemical and ancient sunlight, glistering,
past the pyrites, with possibilities of gold, and performing
endless miracles of photosynthesis. Another essay from
the same collection, 'The Return', whose ostensible opening subject is the apparently unpromising one of four
wooden nesting-boxes put up before the same War, and
what has happened to them since, modulates into the
same aureate theme:

Thinking of spring, in childhood the eyes would brim, a little
pain would steal into the heart. The birds were far away; they
would return, but those former springtimes were gone for ever,
although we would wander in the same meadow, hear the same
mingling of song, breathe the same sweet wander-wind. Even
so, it would never be the same again; and the poignancy of the
thought almost stopped the heart beating. Ancient sunlight![5]

We are to meet the golden strands again and again,
throughout *The Flax of Dream*, the minor works, and the
Chronicle. Purging, purificatory, purgatorial, this sunlight sometimes images a lost and aching happiness whose
sources are in paradise; sometimes even more painfully,
the principle of Truth: Truth resurrected, Truth's corpse
revived out of spiced and fragrant ashes. The final cry of
the *Chronicle*'s closing volume, *The Gale of the World*, is
' "O my friends! My friends in ancient sun-
light!" ';[6] and here is the marvellous version of the same
lament from *The Golden Virgin*:

Come back, he [Phillip Maddison] cried wildly in his mind,
come back, O summer day of my childhood, let me re-enter
just one crystal moment; but he could see nothing, all was
beyond invisibility, far away in ancient sunlight, life lost for

evermore. For the moment he felt stricken into stone; then turning away, walked out of the park between the avenue of chestnuts planted, Gran'pa had said, in Charles the Second's time.[7]

The conclusion of the passage quoted is not, as may at first appear, bathetic. It is with such numb recollections of 'the ancientness and continuity of life'[8] that the spirit sensitive to history, as Henry Williamson everywhere showed himself to be, sustains itself when stricken into stone. Out of the rock is building made; petrifaction, petrification, can produce sculpture; so, indeed, may the process of freezing, as it did for Phillip Maddison:

. . . the north-east wind brought snow, and in the morning the entire landscape was white, and the tops of the beeches in the plantation north of the field arose above a white cliff. The wind had carved it with flowing lines of sculpture. . . . More snow fell at night. No stars were to be seen; he was entirely shut off in a world soundless but for the slight falling sighs of the flakes of snow.[9]

A like landscape is revealed to Wilbo in *The Phasian Bird*:

Again the wind was drifting as the spirit of ice over water and land, the snow streaming as spectral smoke with the moving airs. Drifts increased under the eddies of the wind, where flakes rested tranquil in the hollows of movement. Brambles that during the years had overgrown fallen gates and posts, in tangled over-arching from uncut hedges, were filled with snow. The horse-plow on the headland was smoothed of its framed purpose, becoming as a hulk of snow with broken spars, ensculped and emblanched above the frozen waves of furrows. Each tree trunk in the Carr [a wood planted as a covert for game birds] was moulded oval by the snow clinging to windward, as the clear air poured in from the north-east.[10]

The stories, articles, essays and prose fragments that together make up *The Lone Swallows*, and the tales that constitute such volumes as *The Peregrine's Saga* and *The Old Stag*, are not of equal weight or merit. Some are pot-boilers, and show the accompanying fatigue. But how-ever variously constructed the individual units — these light, airy, delicate as lace, those coarse and crude, with hessian heaviness and loosely-strung — the size of the in-terstices is always deliberate. Exquisitely formed of moss, lichen, fluff and feathers, the nest of chaffinch or wren is not meant to accommodate the untidy crow. What, writ-ten against time, may seem in a miscellany flung together with similar desperation by a publisher bitty will appear in its true light when properly placed, occupying its true function. In an isolated newspaper-article, the exaltation of the brown seed, not yet known to be capable of flower-ing, found on a grimy pavement near the Thames, of 'a sort of dandelion that I sought', the Yellow Goatsbeard or John-go-to-bed-at-noon, into 'A lovely disk of gold, a summer day, a wandering bee, . . . more valuable than a gold ring'[11] may seem not only extravagant but embar-rassing; yet few would deny the plant's progeny a magical status who can appreciate the masterly *Dandelion Days*. Imagination flourishes, reaping a harvest of memory, in deserts where seed fail. As much as Blake's Sun-flower is our author's dandelion a talisman to the 'sweet golden clime' of possibly irrecoverable paradise.

To protest against oceans, to complain against a range of mountains, such as the Himalayas, that they are form-less would be foolish. Also it would be false. They exhibit in their grandeur a superabundance of forms, and of Form. Mountains will appear differently according as we view them from their base, their pinnacle or another planet, and as we bring to them the eyes of a geologist, meteorologist, miner, explorer, aviator or poet:

The snow drifted to the earth, each flake a unique pattern, varying with angle and form of line. The snowflakes were of frozen water, and clear as water, but the diversity of angle and facet reflected rays of light as infinite as the designs of leaf and frond of green nature. Thus the white light was returned to the sky, and men said the snow was white.[12]

The landscape of *The Beautiful Years* is an idyllic one: a 'sweet countryside whose beauty of dream-flax, though fail faith in friend and love of maid, is ever for those who would weave it.'[13] Moving from it into *A Chronicle of Ancient Sunlight* is like coming, unprepared, upon Guernica, or — what preparation could there be? — looking, mute and wordless, at the first newsreels out of Belsen, the first photographs of the dreadful fungoid growth above Hiroshima since whose eruption men have mostly mislaid the power to weep for what they do, and in the weeping, care.

'Human kind cannot bear very much reality,' said another of the agonists, the voices of conscience, of his age.[14] Like other great male writers — Wordsworth, Dickens, Tolstoy — Henry Williamson insisted upon telling hurtful truths, and took upon himself the duty of being at times massively boring that this entails. Without much gift of persuasion, in a tempestuous season he ordered a reluctant audience to think about things requiring of them too much effort, from the contemplation of which they naturally preferred to shy away. When lack of response indicated deafness, resistance, or such apathy as must have seemed to him deranged, he repeated himself, sometimes at increased volume and (since repetition is tiring, shouting into a whirlwind wrecks the voice, and additions may enervate) somewhat subdued urgency. He was in consequence accused (justly?) of ranting; but his detractors' basic quarrel was less with his manner than his matter: the triple argument that worship of the Golden Calf must cease; that uncreative minds must stop destroying creative ones; and that when men of different nations

treat one another as human beings (which is recom-
mended in the Scriptures and called in wartime fraternization) there will no longer be an enemy or a war.
Intensely patriotic, tortured by scruples only 'the passionate few' could understand, he was occasionally mistaken — traditional fate of patriots — for a traitor, because
he dared to assert what perhaps one day will seem incon-
trovertible: that by denying to the German people all
humanity in our propaganda, we held equal responsibil-
ity with the Nazi leaders for the creation of a Dachau.

His structure is not that of madrigals and miniatures
but of murals, oratorios, symphonies. As with a cathedral, while to appreciate the stonemason's or the
glazier's craft it is necessary to examine minutely the
tiniest details, each jutty, frieze, and coign of vantage
where the swallow breeds, evaluation of the art, the
architecture, will involve standing back, looking up, and
responding with awe to the immensity of the vaulting.
The style of Henry Williamson is the style of grandilo-
quence, exerting little appeal for those petty critics who,
in the words of a writer he loved and often quoted, 'could
never see a literary bough project beyond the trim level of
the day but they must lop it with a crooked criticism.'[15]
Among composers the closest analogy for his most shapely
works might be with Delius or Vaughan Williams, while
the more turgid recall the rumbling *Leitmotiven*, clues to
an obsession, of Wagner; or, more recently, the turbulent
and noisy violence of Havergal Brian. Among writers he
resembles Romain Rolland, who was similarly controversial for similar reasons, and author of a similarly magnificent, similarly flawed *roman-fleuve*, sinewy and ornery,
as well as of a pamphlet considered seditious because it
attempted to prevail upon the aggressive to become
pacific.

An ocean, a mountain-range, presents its views
because it can do no other; not for it to make life easier

for boats bobbing on the waves or travellers toiling up the heights.

A range is not a plateau. It contains many a chasm, many an abyss. It has its peaks, pastures, pitfalls, valleys. The present essay sets out to describe some of the scenery below the summit, with occasional cautious glances at what lies beyond, endeavouring to detect the thermals where the kestrel hovers; to espy the worm's-eye view; and to observe—if it can do so without ruffling feathers, putting out the divine flame or risking ruin in precipitate mortality—the fabled nest of the phoenix.

*   *   *   *

Schools and academies may attempt to train him, but the artist remains an autodidact. His education is lifelong. Thus it was with Henry Williamson: 'Shakespeare, Hardy, Shelley, Conrad, Jefferies, Barbusse, Duhamel . . . these and others were my constant companions of the mind as I walked alone by the sea and the hills, and read at night before my solitary hearth by the light of a solitary candle.'[16] Amid the yellow haze of that 'upright, solitary candleflame',[17] in a scene out of grotesque first limned in *The Adelphi*, and transfigured for the purposes of fiction in *The Gale of the World*,[18] Henry Williamson's sons were egged on to emulate the call of a lovesick owl; from the same fantastical glimmer he was himself, winter's wizard, magus of the moonlight as sorcerer of the sun, to conjure up the image of a lone robin, resuscitator of the dead:

In the morning a few chinking notes would tremble on the air . . . throughout the icy solitude of winter his thin candle-gleams of song flickered . . . through the dark lifelessness of the garden. . . .[19]

The writer to whom the robin sang was intensely literary: one, that is, who loved literature instead of hating it as those publishers' readers do who cannot abide quotation and think 'fine writing' self-evidently deserves a sneer. Already he kept, in his teens, a journal, transcribed as 'A Boy's Nature Diary' in *The Lone Swallows*, that shows his early happiness in, and knowledge of, the habits and the habitats of birds, and was to be transmuted into the *Diary of Nature Observations*, alias *Official Diary of Observations*, in *Dandelion Days*. To the acuity of observation which underlay his peculiar talent for onomatopoeic representation of the language of animals and birds,[20] and compressed itself into such magistral phrases as 'the fleeing specks of the swallows',[21] he added stores of information garnered from the pages of Richard and Cherry Kearton's *British Birds*.[22] Then there came the 1914-18 War and its lasting trauma. Like Willie Maddison he 'knew every flower, bird, fern, grass, rock, animal, bush; and the vain and empty sky over all.'[23] He suffered something like a death of the cordial spirit. 'God so loved the world that he tortured Jesus Christ'.[24] We may assume from numerous references and allusions in his work that his discovery of the dead writer who was to effect his own spiritual rebirth closely resembled that described in the *persona* of Willie Maddison in *The Pathway*:

'. . . Being a coward, I died a thousand deaths during the War; in fact, I died altogether, and in December, 1918, coming home to be demobilized . . . I happened to go into a bookshop at Dover, and saw a copy of Jefferies' *Story of My Heart*. . . . I opened it and glanced at it: I read one sentence, and in that moment was changed: all the stored impressions of my boyhood seemed to return, with a mysterious spirit that brought the tears to my eyes many times as I read on . . .'[25]

The inspiring spirit was both wild and gentle. Less gregarious than Thoreau, with a sharper intellect than Shelley, Richard Jefferies became a rebel against material values, a visionary more lucid than Blake. He was neither a pantheist, nor, in his own estimation, a deist. Again and again, however, there recur in his works incandescent expressions of admiration for a symbolically pagan Sun-god he called, after the Egyptians, Sesostris which, combined with mistier evocations of the ambiguous 'something far more deeply interfused' of which Wordsworth had transcendent glimpses, resulted in that worship of ancient sunlight wherein Henry Williamson was enthusiastically to steep himself.

Jefferies' prose was plain, sweet, lyrical and true, marred only by a slight overfondness for inversion of subject and verb, for archaism of vocabulary, and for one irregularity of syntax (the Fowlerian 'fused participle') which becomes in his hands very nearly a virtue. Such a sentence as 'Looking now more closely on the snow, the tracks of hares and rabbits that have crossed and recrossed the ice are visible'[26] must offend purist and pedagogue alike; it is not the track of rabbit or hare, but the narrator, who does the looking; yet—editors and publishers please note—to correct the grammar by any of the usual means would be to lose that unique, indefinable sense of the unseen, sympathetic presence watching as if through the foliage of a particular tree that so oddly and so hauntingly imbues Jefferies' vignettes.

Williamson, like all new disciples, imitated the dominie's faults slavishly, and to this influence must be attributed the not infrequent 'Came the dawn' tinge and the broken-backed sentences, like a loved gun, 'pitted and rufoused with rust',[27] that goes off at half-cock, disfiguring the writings of his immaturity. Yet the one-eyed man is well-equipped for battle in the country of the blind—not least if he owns a monocular Zeiss glass captured at Bullecourt. It was from Jefferies that he gained the strength to go on at all. From Jefferies also did he learn to combine scrupulous exactitude in dispassionate delineation of the individual with passionate espousal of the soul of a species.

Rebirth came from fire. Gunfire was remembered in sunlight, a fallen comrade in flames from the felling of an ancient tree. Henry Williamson worked for most of his life in the 'small hut built years ago of oak, straw, plaster, and elmwood'[28] of which he said in his *Indian Summer Notebook*:

All late spring and summer the hut lies within a dark green shade. One needs a fire there when writing, even on a hot day, for the act of imaginative creation draws strength from the body: cold sweats accompany the flow of images being turned into word symbols.[29]

Despite his prolific output, much of the energy went into revision, which required

tenacity to learn, to unlearn, to discard, to tear up, to rewrite, to recast, to screw up and hurl into a large wastepaper basket, to start again, to cross out, to alter, to begin once more, to scrap yet another time and to persevere through much self-dismay and hopelessness. . . .[30]

The whole of *Tarka the Otter* was rewritten seventeen times, and one of its chapters more than thirty.[31] In this exhausting, ritualistic, reiterated sacrifice may lie another of the origins of the recurrent phoenix image. There could be several more; we have already glimpsed the warming of the refrigerated heart; but in a receptacle no loftier than wastepaper basket or dustbin there may nestle the vital egg. The artistic imagination works upon dross, dry cinders, bearing out of the rubbish heap a golden flame.

I do not wish to go into the vexed question of the degree to which Henry Williamson's or any other author's characters may be identified with aspects of himself, except to say—for it is the journalists' preserve—that so far as protagonists are concerned Prufrock's response perhaps suffices, while Polonius has more to him than some producers think:

No! I am not Prince Hamlet, nor was meant to be;
Am an attendant lord, one that will do
To swell a progress, start a scene or two,
Advise the prince; no doubt, an easy tool . . .
Almost, at times, the Fool.[32]

It is, however, pertinent, since Henry Williamson was the author of *The Phoenix Generation*, and his creature or creation Phillip Maddison the author of *The Phoenix*, that in *It Was the Nightingale* Phillip, whose second wedding 'had all passed in a haze of unreality, like nearly everything in his life to do with people',[33] both sees himself as a phoenix and compares his second wife to 'a falcon flying to the aid of a tiercel with eyasses, whose mate had been shot'[34]—male bird thus resembling that tiercel whose flight is so superbly portrayed in *The Scandaroon*:

The bird was using the west wind which, rebounding against the air below the Hole, flowed up the precipice in streams of varying velocity. The tiercel, slipping through mixed uprising jets of air, and *falling* against the flow, had risen in mastery of the wind's force. I fancy the bird had had no sensation of being lifted: wave, rock, green sward and enemy man had merely become smaller until it was hanging poised in the wind which poured past its eyes.[35]

Being self-begotten out of elemental fire, the phoenix can have no true mate. In *The Phasian Bird*, Chee-kai, the Chinese pheasant (*phasianus reevesii, phasianus veneratus*) that was brought over by the Romans from the Colchian strand, and from whose avatar another origin of the phoenix myth may derive, is reared by the cock-partridge Pertris and dies unpaired, or paired only in death with an unlikely companion, Harra the Dench-man, otherwise the hooded crow. We may set beside this complexity that in *The Innocent Moon*, where

As he [Phillip Maddison] watched, greatly excited, a finch came from over the streaky, smashing sea, a frail dark mite flit-tering to reach the shore and sanctuary. The smaller per-egrine, the tiercel or male, saw it, tipped up, shot down . . . and missed! — He felt terror, as though the finch were himself.[36]

Perhaps in the 'Nature' writings Henry Williamson, in-deed, was most himself. His sensibility was rare — both precious and raw, incorrigibly vulnerable. In more than one sense was he his own quarry: he was his mine, rifted sometimes with other authors' ore; and he was the hunted hunter, the scapegoat, the rogue male. He was the bird at which he flew; he was kin with the preying owl and the owl's prey. His hunting stories were strong meat. He knew the red fox's rank smell. He had run with the hare and ridden with the hounds, cried with the pack as well as desired the gallant buck's escape. His depiction of that aristocratic beast is down-to-earth and mordant, a world away from the charming sentimentalism of Felix Salten's *Bambi*:

Strong-necked and content, the stag walks down the rows of growing turnips, gripping one with his teeth, pulling it from the earth, and jerking his bite free with a toss of his head. . . . The stag is like the pre-revolution Turk: he is entirely selfish, and guards a harem in the rutting season, including all the hinds his strength can gain for him in combat with rivals.[37]

Yet few could equal in tenderness Henry Williamson's description of the activity of 'Inoffensive worms':[38]

earth worms, their whole bodies sensitive to light, were out of their holes in the garden beds, and on the lawn, drawing leaves to their tunnels, where in darkness those gentle priests would perform the annual miracle of changing dead tissue into living soil.[39]

Here it might not be entirely fanciful to suggest that 'annual', with its resemblance to 'annular', and in association with 'priests', evokes both the rings on the worms' writhing bodies, and that other ring, worth less though it may be than the golden dandelion, with which the marital ceremony is performed.

* * * *

'There are insensitive men and sensitive men, and sometimes the most sensitive are at times the most self-tortured, and therefore torturing. Objects of hate are but our own chimaerae. They arise from wounds within us. So we seek scapegoats, to void our hurts.'[40]

When the part of life that involves people is 'a haze of unreality', fitful as candlelight, small wonder if the 'spirit unappeased and peregrine'[41] should be drawn especially to birds,

> *that fill their breasts*
> *But with each other and themselves*
> *And their built or driven nests*[42]

nor if it note 'the authentic wing-flicker in the upper air',[43] but, like the kestrel, return its gaze

to where with head bent to focus the stereoscopic sight of its full liquid eyes, it had been observing red and green and blue flashes in the snow.[44]

Whether or not the various Maddisons', and Henry Williamson's, preoccupation with fire originated in 'guilt as yet only superficially recognized',[45] there are lessons to be learned from it, as from all suffering, when a protagonist

in curious detachment . . . wonders if he will hear himself screaming in the black-billowing and impenetrable bright flames . . . the heat that breaks as with phoenix-claws the small clearness of self from the charred diminished body.[46]

Lucifer; Eosphoros; *Prolix praecox*, bird of dawning, or phoenix of revival? 'In my end is my beginning':[47]

Glancing backwards at the swirl and scream of black-headed gulls following the bright breasts of the twin-plows reversing the surface of the earth, the impression given was of clamant and winged turbulence immediately behind resolving into a series of broken white spirals coiling off up-screwing furrows. Looking more particularly, the driver saw how each bird of many hundreds made its approach to the new-turned soil. Each gull as it alighted, with upheld tremulous wings and red mouth open to scream its excitement, ran along the furrow, jostling with others to pull at worm or grub only a few inches off the shine of travelling steel.[48]

'Only a man harrowing clods';[49] we, the clods he harrowed? Time, all his progeny, will tell.

And if, arrived at ultra and beyond,
You find yourself in no strange land,
Accept, though they be both foolish and fond,
These notes, my master, of a 'prentice hand.

NOTES

1. Richard Jefferies, *The Story of My Heart: My Autobiography*, Longmans, Green, Pocket Library edition (1907), reprinted 1911, page 190.

2. Richard Jefferies, *The Gamekeeper at Home* and *The Amateur Poacher*, World's Classics edn, single volume, 1948, p.352.
3. Henry Williamson, 'Four Elegies: Boy', *The Lone Swallows and Other Essays of Boyhood and Youth*, Putnam (1922), limited edn, illustrated C. F. Tunnicliffe (1945), repr. March 1948, pp.49-50.
4. ibid., p.50.
5. 'The Return', op. cit., p.146.
6. *The Gale of the World*, Macdonald, 1969, p.361.
7. *The Golden Virgin*, Macdonald (1957), third impression, 1966, pp.419-20.
8. 'Peregrines in Love', *The Lone Swallows*, ed. cit., p.17.
9. *The Phoenix Generation* (Macdonald, 1965), Panther revised edn, 1967, pp.153-4.
10. *The Phasian Bird*, Faber and Faber, mcmxlviii, pp. 16-17.
11. 'London Papers: A Seed in Waste Places', *The Lone Swallows*, ed. cit., pp.157, 158.
12. *The Phasian Bird*, p.16.
13. *The Beautiful Years*, Faber and Faber, edn of mcmlxvii, p.64.
14. T. S. Eliot, *Murder in the Cathedral*, Part II. Cf. *Burnt Norton*.
15. Francis Thompson, 'Shelley', in *The Works of Francis Thompson*, Vol. III: Prose; Burns and Oates, n.d., p.15.
16. Henry Williamson, General Introduction to *Collected Nature Stories*, Macdonald and Jane's, 1970, p.11, and cf. *Lucifer Before Sunrise*, Macdonald, 1967, p.206.
17. 'Words on the West Wind', *The Adelphi*, Vol. 25, No. 2, January-March 1949, p.68.
18. *The Gale of the World*, pp.257 ff.
19. *The Beautiful Years*, ed. cit., p.179.
20. e.g. hens 'squark', a young female rook 'squaks', otters 'tiss'.
21. 'The Lone Swallows', in vol. of same title, ed. cit., p.9.
22. See Henry Williamson, 'The Last Summer', *Sunday Times* colour supplement, 2 August 1964.
23. *The Pathway*, Faber and Faber, edn of 1969, p.362.

24. *The Dream of Fair Women*, Faber and Faber, edn of mcmlxviii, p.133.
25. *The Pathway*, ed. cit., p.228.
26. Richard Jefferies, *The Amateur Poacher*, ed. cit., p.337.
27. *The Beautiful Years*, ed. cit., p.138.
28. 'Words on the West Wind', p.67.
29. *Indian Summer Notebook*, Part II, *Evening Standard*, 17 November 1964.
30. 'Notes of a 'Prentice Hand', *The Adelphi*, loc. cit., pp.114-15.
31. Eleanor Graham, 'How the Book Came to be Written', in Henry Williamson, *Tarka the Otter: His Joyful Water-Life and Death in the Two Rivers* (1927), Penguin Books (1937), repr. with revisions and map, 1963, p.10.
32. T. S. Eliot, *The Love Song of J. Alfred Prufrock*.
33. Henry Williamson, *It Was the Nightingale*, Macdonald, 1962, p.338.
34. ibid., p.335.
35. *The Scandaroon*, Macdonald, 1972, p.92.
36. *The Innocent Moon*, Macdonald, 1961, p.184.
37. *The Wild Red Deer of Exmoor: A Digression on the Logic and Ethics and Economics of Stag-Hunting in England Today*, Faber and Faber, 1931, p.43. The book is dedicated to the gentle reader.
38. 'A Weed's Tale', *The Peregrine's Saga and other Wild Tales*, in *Collected Nature Stories*, p.49.
39. *The Power of the Dead* (Macdonald, 1963), Panther revised edn, 1966, p.314.
40. *The Golden Virgin*, ed. cit., p.75. The speaker is Father Aloysius.
41. T. S. Eliot, *Little Gidding*.
42. Robert Frost, 'The Hill Wife'.
43. *Lucifer Before Sunrise*, Macdonald, 1967, p.223.
44. *The Phasian Bird*, p.27.
45. *The Gale of the World*, p.299. The theory is undermined by its attribution to the Diaphanist, of dubious qualification.
46. *The Gale of the World*, p.170.
47. T. S. Eliot, *East Coker*.

48. *The Phasian Bird*, pp.188-9. See also *Lucifer Before Sunrise*, pp. 356, 380.
49. Thomas Hardy, *In Time of 'The Breaking of Nations'*.

HENRY WILLIAMSON: WITNESS OF THE GREAT WAR

Hugh Cecil

AS the Great War of 1914-18 has receded from living memory, and the last survivors among the 'men who really did the job' are becoming scarcer, the appetite to understand their experience grows much stronger, and the last ten years have seen a spate of the culled reminiscences of the still living. This comes at a time, too, when the official records are being thrown open and historians are studying intensively the forces that took the nations of Europe into war, and the ambitions, motives and organisational ideas of those who ran the war effort at home and at the fighting fronts. In such a study of a major historical field a knowledge of the atmosphere and sensibilities of the period, at all levels, is crucial. For this, the literature of the Great War—fiction, poetry and personal recollection—provides a vital tool.

Innumerable reminiscences and novels about the First World War have been written. Anyone who is prepared to browse their way painstakingly through the shelves full of mouldering books in the second hand bookshops will almost certainly be rewarded by finding half a dozen volumes at each visit; of these most will be works now long forgotten, if they ever made much impact. Few deserve a better fate—though all are of use to those interested in the impact of war on individual lives and in the personal interpretations that contemporaries put on their experience of the period.

A dozen or so names stand out among English authors: some, like Robert Graves, Edmund Blunden, Frederic Manning, Siegfried Sassoon, V. M. Yeates, Guy Chapman, Cecil Lewis (I speak here only of prose works) rightly so; others, less so, like Richard Aldington, R. H. Mottram and C. E. Montague, whose reputation is higher, to this day, than is commensurate with their real talents as war writers. There are many authors who have passed from great popular acclaim to near oblivion — Wilfred Ewart, with his *Way of Revelation*, and Robert Keable, with his *Simon Called Peter*, for example; and who now is familiar with the war works of Richard Blaker, Edward Thompson, Warwick Deeping, Ronald Gurner, or C. R. Benstead? Poets have lasted better; but I do not intend to talk of them here.

Among this host of brilliant and less able authors Henry Williamson stands out. Yet his name as a war writer is not as well known as it should be. The richness of his imagination, his lucid and often beautiful prose style, and the extraordinary wealth of human and inhuman detail make him a thoroughly rewarding author for the general reader and the social historian of the War alike. It is not the purpose of this essay to investigate why his contribution in this field has been so little acknowledged. Even Paul Fussell in his original and widely researched *The Great War and Modern Memory* gives him no outstanding attention. It may be that those who are not drawn to Williamson's works on country life and natural history — for which he is most commonly known — have thereby failed to give themselves the chance to progress to his interpretations of the First World War. Whatever the explanation, it is vital that the neglect should be remedied. In the pages that follow I intend to lay out some reasons why Williamson's record in particular should commend itself to the historian and why he deserves to be remembered far more than many other writers who were soldiers in the same struggle.

In the first place there have been few other authors writing over a long span of time who have been so pre-occupied with the War. In only six of his major works does the actual experience of combat form the main theme—in *The Patriot's Progress* and the five wartime volumes of the *Chronicle of Ancient Sunlight*. The event has also a central importance in the *Flax of Dream* novel-sequence and in much of his very largely autobiographi-cal work on other subjects the after effects of the War play a dominant part: in *The Sun in the Sands* and *The Gold Falcon*, for example. In *The Wet Flanders Plain* (1929), Williamson describes his postwar pilgrimage to the battlefields in Belgium, recollects the war years and appeals for a fresh spirit of international understanding. And time and again there are recollections and allusions to that past—as in his account of farming days in Nor-folk, in his short story about a starving vixen caught in a trap, in his book on Richard Jefferies, to mention but a few instances. He could and did deliberately turn away from his obsession in some of his literary endeavours. But the psychic wounds and the stimulus to the imagination were alike too deep for it ever to fade. This being so, he was able to handle the theme of war late in life without time having diminished its intensity for him. Indeed his readers have gained, for in the *Chronicle*, the first volume of which did not appear until 1951, his percep-tions had deepened and his skills developed.

Most of those who recounted their war memories did so within the ten or fifteen years after 1918. This was part of the process of recovery—to get the horror out of their system and to make money. Some wrote very much with the market in mind; first, in the years immediately following the Armistice, when there was still a place for the heroic style of novel in which the War formed a suit-able setting for the kind of cliché-ridden melodrama of love, rejection, ordeal and triumph which was very popular before 1914 and during the War. Wilfred Ewart's *Way of Revelation* is a case in point. As time went on — the change was not abrupt — writers began to dare to say rather more about the unglamorous and the ignoble sides of the experience. This 'disenchanted' genre became increasingly fashionable, epitomised, in the '30s, by works like the embittered, and surprisingly modern, *War is War* by '*Ex-Private X*', in which the author on one occasion explains his lack of fear by the fact that he was preoccupied at the time by his trousers falling down. The runaway success of Remarque's vulgar and meretricious *All Quiet on the Western Front* was part of this vogue. Paul Fussell has reminded us how Robert Graves himself admitted that he slanted his account with sales in mind, and shows how he actually did introduce falsehood into the picture he gave.

A leading theme, also, of Fussell's thought-provoking, though sometimes misleading, work is that writers at the time were still too much caught up in the literary traditions and preoccupations of the pre-War 'innocent era' to give a completely truthful picture — however much they might wish to do so. Experience was filtered through an earlier vision of life which lacked the vocabulary and metaphors to state it in the stark obscene terms that were required. A gentler sentiment and a more romantic language than we use today inevitably softened the impacts of their narratives, with very few exceptions. Possibly Fussell has overstated his case. His misunderstanding of the British sensibility — in Edwardian times and today — and his minor inaccuracies, lead him to conclusions and comparisons which are not wholly valid. Nonetheless his point generally is an important one; and it is particularly interesting to look at Henry Williamson in that light.

In 1930 Williamson published his first war novel, *The*

Patriot's Progress. Although he did not deliberately make his creation to suit a market, it formed part of a 'publisher's package' which put constraints on him. He was asked to write the book round the linocuts of William Kermode, who at his request added further pictures to fit a plot which Williamson had in mind. It is a story of 'Everysoldier' at war and is vividly and precisely told. It has a 'disenchanted' theme—perhaps inevitable at the time. The protagonist, John Bullock, is an honest, simple soldier whose patriotism and trust of his superiors lead him deeper into nightmare; the final irony is that he escapes from the hell of conflict only by becoming a useless, mutilated hulk, whose innocent heroism is a matter of indifference after the War. Though it is full of Williamson's fire and sensitive observation, *The Patriot's Progress* seems now too much of a literary creation and its conclusions glib and unoriginal. Except in mastery of prose it does not stand out among the better war novels of its day. Williamson himself had two objections to it: 'the thought of it,' he recalled, 'helped to delay my own books on the War.' He added: 'on re-reading the book I found it mannered to the anti-staff period of the infantryman's war of 1915-1917. I wanted to write balanced novels; the staff also had their problems.'

The record for Williamson, in other words, was not straight. He had been carried along by a fashionable interpretation which he recognised was only half true. Given time, he was able to escape from the constricting influences of the inter-war period. It may well be, indeed, that his increased isolation in the later '30s and the '40s made it possible for him to develop undisturbed. So that his picture of the War in the *Chronicle* is on the whole far truer to what he actually experienced.

As for Williamson's sensibility, one cannot deny that he did share with many of his contemporaries the late romantic outlook of the Edwardian age. Sometimes this mars the *Chronicle*, often it enhances it. He wished to convey the men's yearning for warmth and light in the midst of horror; and he always saw the German soldier as linked with the British in a brotherhood of suffering. Unfortunately here, however, romantic sentimentality interferes with fidelity to truth. It seems as if he felt he had to include an English equivalent of the *Lili Marlene* of the haunting poem (later, song) written at the Front by a serving soldier, Hans Leip. The result was Lily, in *The Golden Virgin* — touching, warm-hearted, beautiful — the soldier's dream. Naturally such a life-altering personality could not be allowed to interfere for long with his generally faithful account of the War; so Lily was eliminated by Zeppelin attack — statistically an unlikely tragedy. In other respects Williamson's romanticism is not regrettable. The sentiment that he felt about his close companions and his country only reflects what he — and countless others — felt at the time. Moreover, there is plenty of satire and squalor in his accounts to balance it. It is far from the sentiment of an armchair patriot safely removed from actual scenes of battle.

In writing long after the event he was not, of course, unique. He is, however, the most talented author to do so. There have been plenty of recollections by serving soldiers which have been put into anthologies of late. Their impact is moving but repetitive; there is not really very much new in books like *Tommy Goes to War* because many of the contributors were simple, and often uneducated. It is the cumulative effect of these anthologies which makes the impact, rather than the individual imaginations of the writers. Two other recent war reminiscences come to mind: one by Eric Hiscock (1976) which is studiedly cynical, and a novel by Stuart Cloete: *So Young They Died* (1969). This, though based on the author's actual experience of the War, fails to convince. It is hard to believe that it is not the work of a much younger man who has simply cobbled a selection of crude sexual passages together with some conscientious research from old memoirs.

One of Williamson's greatest assets was his astonishing power of observation. The naturalist whose eyes so minutely perceived the ways of animal life saw with the same acuteness man in his wartime habitat, man adapting himself to discomfort, man in a state of rage and fear. His description of going into action for the first time at the battle of Messines on October 31, 1914 cannot be bettered:

With a lingering glance at the tree, as to a friend he must leave for ever, Phillip made himself walk forward with the others, like a man walking through ice giving way before him. With shaking fingers he took a clip of five cartridges from a pouch and wrenched off one. Where to put the other four? For a few moments it was an imponderable problem. Then he thought of his right-hand lower tunic pocket. But it was already full — Civic, matches, pouch, bundle of letters from Mother. With a sob he tore at the contents of the pocket, trying to wrench away a fistful. He threw all away as though his life depended upon it — red rubber Crocodile pouch of Hignett's Cavalier, box of Bryant and May's matches, pipe, talismanic letters. He shrieked at himself in his head as he freed other cartridges of their clips and dropped them in his pocket. Mother, mother!

His life depended on a pocket full of cartridges. But supposing a cartridge still would not feed-in? *Father was right. They should have been given a chance to fire their rifles.* He pulled back the bolt, and at once saw that the spring of the magazine was not strong enough to push the cartridge, already in position, into the chamber. The front stop clips were the wrong shape for pointed ammunition. The pointed end of the bullet would not feed-in level; it tipped up, and when rammed in by the bolt, was sort-of crushed. It was liable to explode like that, quite apart from the jamming.

Removing the magazine, he shook out the remaining

cartridges, and put them in his pocket. Then slipping a round into the barrel, he closed the bolt, and fired it into the air. The butt in recoil struck his cheekbone, for he had been holding the rifle loosely: but the blow was not felt in the wild and trembling frenzy now that he had found out how to load. He looked from left to right, saw the long lines of men as far as the trees, and then with a secondary ice-shock realised that nothing could now save him from what was to happen when he reached the crackle of the skyline.

From Williamson, the historian can gain, as from no other First War writer, a knowledge of the way the men lived — and died — the tobacco they smoked, the food they ate, their superstitions, their prejudices, their battle shock, their machines; and — though his characters are sometimes two-dimensionally drawn — of their conversation and the language they used too. Some of these details can be encountered elsewhere; nowhere are they to be found in such profusion as in the *Chronicle*, making up a total picture of the fighting front which is unsurpassed. And this is not just in his depiction of the fighting in France and Flanders: the Home Front — British daily life at the time — received the same masterly treatment.

In all this there is evidence of something very strong in Williamson — his deep-rooted love of life, which triumphed over self-hating and destructive impulses. It is strange that a man who, probably better than anyone, has described the misery of war — the feelings of being trapped, of panic, of isolation and separation from home, of helplessness and of the endless, relentless discomfort — should nonetheless have been able to say publicly (on a television programme near the time of his 80th birthday) that he had actually enjoyed the War. But one of life's paradoxes is that moments of great fear and sadness are not invariably the times we look back to with the most regret. Not that we wish them back — far from it. But miseries can call out qualities of strength that have otherwise been dormant, and they can give an intensity to life at the time. Williamson's tireless curiosity about his surroundings, even at times of extreme danger, is very impressive, particularly when one considers that he must have suffered inwardly more than most.

One can forgive him some of the cardboard characters and the sometimes unselective and over-long passages, the plagiarism even—he has quite shamelessly lifted whole episodes from Michael Macdonagh's diary: *London in the Great War*—when one sees how total a picture he has built up, extending not just over a wide area of England and the Continent, but before and after the War. With his assistance one has a powerful and convincing impression of the popular mind in England. His political explanations seem often naive and simplistic. But his knowledge of the mentality which led thousands of young men in London to rush to arms, and, all ignorant of realities, to turn their backs on a narrow, boring and depressing life of drudgery—this is deeply convincing. It makes a more significant contribution to our understanding of that still mysterious phenomenon than most of the research which has been pursued to date. His sustained treatment, in the later volumes of the *Chronicle*, of the lingering effects of the War on individuals after the cessation of hostilities is without parallel.

Finally in this brief assessment, one cannot underestimate the personality and background of the leading character, Phillip Maddison, as central to the success of Williamson's account of the War in the *Chronicle*. Phillip Maddison is very young, unstable, wild, self-hating, hypersensitive, imaginative, provocative and given to foolish and irritating pranks. An odd person, it might be said, with whom it could be hard at first to identify oneself. But he has also his more 'ordinary' characteristics—his affectionate friendliness, his capacity for enthusiasm and admiration; his enjoyment of riding—on horses, cycles and motorbikes; his fumbling, often unsuccessful episodes with girls; his displays of undignified high spirits; his social insecurity, his love of public houses, his choice of frequently commonplace companions. A question that almost everybody is bound to ask themselves when reading about a war is 'How would I fare if I was in the same situation?' Faced with the self-confidence of a Robert Graves or the rare refinement and culture of a Siegfried Sassoon—not to mention the latter's privileged position in society—it is hard to imagine oneself quite in their shoes. Likewise 'Everysoldier' figures, like Bullock in *Patriot's Progress*, are too much of an abstraction to imagine oneself having anything but a theoretical common humanity with them. Phillip Maddison, on the other hand, for all his eccentricities, is much more truly 'Everyman' for us today. His background, superficially at least, is prosaic and economically unexceptional. As a child, he plays with the other children in the street, goes to the same school and joins the Scouts with them. There is nothing specially refined or cultivated, though it is worthy and genteel, about his suburban minor middle-class life. In his position in society he feels deferential towards the wealthy and well-connected; at the same time he is uneasy in his attitude towards the working-class people he sees around him, moved by their poverty, but alarmed by their roughness. At the outset of the War he is very much of the 'middling sort'—one of a huge and undistinguished mass; not a gentleman, but respectable. People of his class were prouder and poorer than they are now; in other ways, however, in their lack of inner confidence and certainty, they resemble a large group in society today. In this democratic age it is easier to identify with Phillip Maddison at war than it is with many of those from the upper bourgeoisie, gentry and aristocracy who published their war experiences. It is no particular credit to Henry Williamson as a writer that this should be so. Nonetheless it is an important reason why the *Chronicle*'s war volumes can continue to be valid and convincing to a wide public.

A test of a really good book is the degree to which it repays repeated reading. The war novels of the *Chronicle* sequence, especially the two earlier ones, *How Dear is Life* and *Fox Under My Cloak*, yield more and more with each return to them. They are like memory itself—small, bright, mysterious patches of sunlight, recollected misery and guilt, affection, sense of loss, embarrassment and beauty, with the recent and far past mingling always together. After reading them I had at times the illusion—so intense is Williamson's vision—that I had actually seen the men who marched away in the autumn of 1914 and that even, perhaps, I was among their number. I felt suddenly close to cousins killed at Villers Cotterets and Hooge nearly thirty years before I was born. A writer who can do this to one is going beyond simply shocking, horrifying, moving and informing his readers. He is actually bringing them to share his own thought so that they can see the war as he does, with moments of clear recollection as well as with the mind's confusions and dreams. That is probably as close as a reader can ever get to knowing what it was like to have fought in the Great War.

Williamson has given us a picture of society at war which though ambitious, is not pretentious. One may object to its didactic side, but it is refreshingly free from literary devices or intellectual games. It seems a good deal less contrived and artificial than, for example, Ford Maddox Ford's much admired tetralogy of the War. Williamson served at the front far longer than Ford. Yet where exceptional talent is concerned that is not really the point. If Williamson had been in the trenches for a briefer period he would still have written a profound and convincing work. The fact is that it is not the degree of experience that makes a good war novel but the mind which interprets that experience. Henry Williamson was one of the few writers of great sensitivity to survive the carnage of the First World War.

BIBLIOGRAPHY

Works by Henry Williamson:
(1) From *A Chronicle of Ancient Sunlight* sequence:
  How Dear Is Life (1954); *A Fox Under My Cloak* (1955); *The Golden Virgin* (1957); *Love and the Loveless* (1958); *A Test to Destruction* (1960; Revised edition, 1964).
(2) Other works on the war:
  The Wet Flanders Plain: Thoughts on the European War, 1914-1918 (1929); *A Soldier's Diary of the Great War,* introd. by H. Williamson (1929); *The Patriot's Progress* (with lino-cuts by William Kermode), 1930).
(3) Books with themes turning on the after effects and consequences of the war:
  The Flax of Dream sequence (First book published 1921; the four novels published as one volume, revised, 1936) *The Gold Falcon or the Haggard of Love* (1933; Revised edition 1947); *The Sun in the Sands* (1947). The last seven (postwar) volumes of the *Chronicle.*
(4) Some of the books (from a very large number) in which the war is recollected and considered:
  The Linhay on the Downs (1929); *The Children of Shallowford* (1939): *The Story of a Norfolk Farm* (1941); *Richard Jefferies: Selections of his Work with details of his Life and Circumstances, his Death and Immortality* (1937; Revised edition 1947).

Works by other authors:
(1) Books by authors commented on by Williamson:
  V. M. Yeates, *Winged Victory* (1935 edn. contains a

tribute by Williamson, which appeared also in the 1961 edn. with a further preface by him). The two principal characters in *Winged Victory* are called Cundall and Williamson; Henry Williamson repaid the compliment to his dead friend by introducing Yeates, as the flier Tom Cundall, into the *Chronicle*. He admired Yeates's book more than any other British war novel except Wilfred Ewart's *Way of Revelation* (1921), which impressed him with its theme of spiritual regeneration and the rejection of false values. The book now seems artificial and dated to the point of absurdity, despite the author's genuine combat experience. Williamson also thought well of Henri Barbusse's *Under Fire* (1916, tr. from French 1917), as the first honest statement of the misery and fellowship of the front—though he felt that there was much more to be said than Barbusse attempted. He was disappointed, on the other hand, by Erich Maria Remarque's *All Quiet on the Western Front* (1929, tr. from German 1929 by A. W. Wheen); he disliked its sensational style and its failure to convey more than the sensation of pre-combat fear; loss of fear, during actual combat, which Williamson himself knew, is not, for example, mentioned as something experienced in battle. Williamson does not appear to have singled out his friend Richard Aldington's *Death of a Hero*, which now reads as self-conscious and contrived, though the battle scenes themselves are powerful. Aldington, on the other hand, thought the *Chronicle* absolutely authentic, and defended it against criticism that Phillip Maddison was too idiosyncratic a hero.

Other novels and memoirs of the fighting fronts alluded to above:

Robert Keable, *Simon Called Peter* (1921); C. E. Montague, *Disenchantment* (1922); R. H. Mottram, *The Spanish Farm trilogy* (1927—first vol. 1924); Edmund Blunden, *Undertones of War* (1928); Siegfried Sassoon, *Memoirs of a Fox Hunting Man* (1928—further volumes in the Sherston Trilogy appeared 1930 and

1938); Ford Madox Ford, *A Man Stood Up* (1926—
other volumes in his tetralogy appeared in 1925 and
1926); Robert Graves, *Goodbye to All That* (1929); C.
R. Benstead, *Retreat* (1930); Richard Blaker, *Medal
Without Bar* (1930); Ronald Gurner, *Pass Guard to
Ypres* (1930); Frederic Manning, *Her Privates We*
(1930); 'Ex-Private X', *War is War* (1930); Guy Chapman, *A Passionate Prodigality* (1933); Edward Thompson, *These Men Thy Friends* (1933); Warwick Deeping,
No Hero This (1936); Cecil Lewis, *Sagittarius Rising*
(1936); Stuart Cloete, *So Young They Died* (1969); Eric
Hiscock, *The Bells of Hell Go Ting-a Ling-a Ling*
(1976); Malcolm Brown, *Tommy Goes to War* (1978).

Other reading:
Bernard Bergonzi, *Heroes' Twilight* (1965). Paul
Fussell, *The Great War and Modern Memory* (1975).
Michael Macdonagh, *London in the Great War* (1935).
Readers may be interested to see Williamson's debt to
this leading *Times* reporter by looking at Macdonagh's
diary entries for 9 and 18 November 1914 (*How Dear Is
Life* chs. 27 & 31), 11, 14 & 22 May 1915 (*Fox Under My
Cloaks* chs. 13 & 14), and his account of the crashed
Zeppelin in September 1916 (*Golden Virgin*, L'Envoi.)

HENRY WILLIAMSON:
THE POWER OF THE DEAD

E. W. Martin

TOWARDS the end of the second world war the thoughts
of many English writers turned away from political issues
towards the problems of rebuilding homes and mending
broken bodies. European writers had been opponents of
nazism, fascism, and totalitarianism, for the most part,
and they felt a desperate need to look beyond politics
after all the suffering and destruction. The first world
war with its discreditable Versailles Treaty had created a
void in the hearts of German people, while in Britain
villages and towns had lost good men, and under the
dross of war old values and social attitudes had become
obsolescent.

It was about 1944 that Malcolm Elwin, who was a
friend of Henry Williamson and of mine, wrote an essay
entitled 'Henry Williamson, Novelist and Prophet of
Reconstruction'.[1] I am not sure that the 'prophetic' side
of Williamson was his greatest strength. Perhaps, indeed,
it was his weakness. However that may be, Elwin opens
his account by saying that on Christmas Eve 1914 wiring
parties moved from the frontline trenches. They moved
silently, fearing that any sound would draw to them
bullets or shells from enemy guns. Then the listening
British soldiers heard singing from the German lines.
Williamson, aged about eighteen or nineteen, was one of
the party. As he moved forward a figure approached and
a voice said haltingly: 'Merry Christmas, English friend.'
And the two men shook hands. On the day that followed,

English and German soldiers forgot war and enjoyed Christmas Day in a proper spirit.

The truth about the fraternisation is hazy. How much is enlargement and nostalgia I have no means of knowing. What we do know, and what matters, is that this incident affected the writings and actions of Henry Williamson for the rest of his life.

To understand the mind of any writer one is forced to rely on his published work, his correspondence and diaries. It is also an advantage to have known the man himself over a long period. I knew Henry Williamson — as I knew Malcolm Elwin — for more than a quarter of a century. They were personal friends, and I doubt if it would be possible for me to write about either with objectivity.

Some people have said that Williamson was an enigma, or that he was controversial and difficult. That means he was unusual and did not conform to an acceptable pattern in the mind of gossips. I think all one can do at this stage is to form some sort of framework, to take a brief look, gather together a few facts and answer a few questions, so that we can see the mind of this faun-like man who in some ways resembled his hero, the Wiltshire writer Richard Jefferies. But he was living in a more difficult age. Rural life had altered, and, as with every serious writer, Williamson's mind did mirror in his private universe the issues and inconsistencies of a civilisation in conflict. I suppose conflict is generally a keynote, or a burden, in the career of every creative writer. He is exposed to what the world offers.

Born in the London borough of Lewisham in 1895 Henry Williamson remained very much a man of the twentieth century, coming to adolescence when there was in the minds of the British politicians a sense of uneasiness, a feeling that there would be war with a Kaiser-dominated Germany. As to the time when his dislike of city life and industry matured in his mind I am not sure. Perhaps it derived from experiences in childhood. His father was a bank clerk, and in long conversations over the years I have at times sensed behind early recollections elements of fear and unhappiness. As yet it would be mistaken to write too much about his personal life. There are those who could be hurt, if hurt should come from the telling. Also, there is no need. In the things that matter he can readily be defended against attack. Yet I know that in Georgeham, Braunton, Barnstaple and elsewhere nothing will safeguard his reputation against interest or even the malice of those who were fascinated by the man whose personality will be associated permanently with the towns, villages and moors that border his favourite rivers, the Taw and the Torridge. To define the 'Henry Williamson country' in a more precise way would be to narrow his region. His mind would stray into strange paths, but the best of this man was bound up with the area he knew best and could never desert.

I believe that any student anxious to write a thesis on the work of a West Country author might think of Henry Williamson as a subject. His place in rural literature is assured, but rural literature itself has been neglected. Dr. Glen Cavaliero, in a careful and notable book on this theme, says: 'The reputation of Henry Williamson is a good example of the divorce between academic and popular standards: a writer of manifest and serious dedication, he has received scant notice in literary history, while enjoying a steady reputation among educated readers as a major and neglected figure.'[2]

To get at the truth, in the course of time, about this impassioned and sometimes prejudiced man will be an uphill task even for his biographer Richard Williamson, who has a full knowledge of the obstacles. The reasons for academic neglect are probably not rooted in controversy. But it is possible that potential writers of theses were frightened of the sheer bulk of the material. Of course, Williamson did live uneasily. He was always worried about work, and there was in him an inner insecurity, so that occasionally he would turn on an admirer who, unknowingly, touched a sensitive nerve. So I reach out cautiously to renew my own acquaintance with a friend who, in life, was sometimes insubstantial and out of reach. A search into this mind — described by our mutual friend the late Kenneth Allsop as one of the most interesting minds of the twentieth century — will go on over the years. The arguments about his beliefs, attitudes and allegiances might outlast the time when any chance of recording an approximation to the truth has faded. On the whole, I believe this truth to be uncomplicated. Or so it seems now, as one glances at what has become a historical record.

To get a proper understanding of the facets of Williamson's mind it is necessary to think about the impulses that force writers to be active, individualistic, outside the herd. Writers during the first world war were different in their political aims from those who marshalled themselves into a powerful international force in the second. The reasons behind literary expression are personal. It is this which leads writers to be a special group, able to talk freely among themselves but not anxious to speak of work (or other writers) outside the circle of professional authors.

In a contribution to a very brief symposium on reasons for writing, the critic V. S. Pritchett said that 'from the social point of view writers exist to show the inconvenience of human nature; just as from the private point of view they enlarge human nature's knowledge of itself.'[3] Writers alone could supply answers. They could not always react in ways that gained general approval.

The second world war did mark a definite increase in the social and political awareness of writers and poets.

There was a deeper commitment and wider involvement because the threats seemed to be more generalised, directed more toward a domination of mind and will. Hatred of tyranny had become almost universal in Europe as the nineteen thirties advanced and as the nazi jackboot crashed into the lives and liberties of so many. That remarkable editor and encourager of talent John Lehmann, himself a writer of distinction, said in a survey first published in 1940 that poets and prose writers had become more aware of 'great social, political and moral changes going on around them', and that they were convinced that they had to communicate truths not uttered by writers during the first world war, who were not in contact with the class-war going on around them in a latent form.[4]

Five years younger than Williamson, Pritchett[5] was very much aware of the political concerns, the deep divisions, the vacillations of some conservative politicians in opposing the nazi war strategy. The menace of totalitarianism increased with the growth of Hitler's Nazi Party from 1933. The social bond and the opposition to ideas likely to menace the individual were well understood by Pritchett and Lehmann, but they also had to lay stress on the need for a freedom of utterance, the privilege of inconvenience. Writers who followed their own vision, true or false, would always be at odds with those who had no vision. Although freedom was the object and democracy its framework, it was this very flexibility that 'the public' resented and tended to obstruct. In a battle for freedom and democracy free speech was 'treachery', and a formal statement of honest belief might become 'treason' under the harsh and protective conditions of war. Those who could not conform were penalised in those periods when a country anxious for peace was drawn into the war's corrupt vortex. In the end, Britain had no choice but to oppose Hitler's territorial demands by force.

Writers like Ezra Pound and P. G. Wodehouse have been defended for their indiscretions in wartime; and this is my intention regarding Henry Williamson, caught up in the sort of atmosphere I have described: that spiritual wasteland between 1918 and 1939. Valiant George Orwell thought it expedient to argue the case for the pathetic Wodehouse when he was publicly attacked for his broadcasts on the German radio.[6] The incidents were no doubt minor, but the mud stuck to him as it did to Pound and Williamson. Wodehouse's books were withdrawn from libraries for a time, and the sales of Williamson's books undoubtedly suffered.

Orwell was keenly interested in politics, and he was often looking at the writer's vocation in the same manner adopted by Pritchett. Orwell believed serious writers were more self-centred than journalists who wrote for money. Self-regard was a powerful stimulus, as were aesthetic enthusiasms, historical impulses, and political purposes.[7] All these factors played their part in Henry Williamson's armoury.

For many British scholars and writers the Spanish Civil War was a watershed. Its horrors forced them to take sides. The Left was now even more sharply divided from the Right. The figure of Franco is as entitled to his place in any historical Chamber of Horrors as Hitler or his jackal, Mussolini. Some British writers like Ralph Fox, John Cornford, Christopher Caudwell, Julian Bell, and many more, lost their lives for the Republican cause. Only a minority stood by Franco. Orwell was troubled by the savagery, and wrote a short poem voicing his perplexity, from which the following is a stanza:

> I dreamed I dwelt in marble halls
> And woke to find it true;
> I wasn't born for an age like this;
> Was Smith? Was Jones? Were you?

Orwell had soon learned that he had to make a stand against a tide that might engulf civilisation. He was not in any sense a pacifist or conscientious objector, although he had no enthusiasm for military trappings, and did not like the braying of the dogs of war slavering for their prey. But he was firm in his affirmation: 'Every line of serious work I have written since 1936, has been written, directly or indirectly, *against* totalitarianism and *for* democratic Socialism, as I understand it. It seems to me nonsense, in a period like our own, to think that one can avoid writing of such subjects. Everyone writes of them in one guise or another. It is simply a question of which side one takes and what approach one follows.'[8]

This seems like a very fair formulation of the kind of background against which Williamson lived and worked. He did not stand where Orwell stood. He was a member of the opposition. It is not possible to judge his work fairly without reference to his political naivety, and without always bearing in mind the long-term effects the 1914 Christmas fraternisation had on his idealistic imagination. For Williamson the choices could never be easy because there was much in his make-up of the romantic, the conservative, and the reactionary.

In a brief account of his work and thought it is easy to misrepresent and offend. Those nearest to him will know that at difficult times in his life he sought my advice on literary and personal problems, even though I was many years his junior. At these times I learned about enduring influences. He was not like the rest of the figures who had expressed distaste for the first world war. He can't be compared, in his reactions, to poets like Robert Graves or Siegfried Sassoon. His attitude was less direct, and his opposition to militarism itself never obtrusive. I suppose he is closer to T. E. Lawrence and the mythology associated with his name. Williamson liked meeting old soldiers. I remember enjoying the way some stood rigidly to attention as they addressed an officer they had known.

Henry Williamson served in the first world war as a private soldier and then as a transport officer. When it was over he had read Richard Jefferies's autobiography, *The Story of My Heart*, which did affect his life. He wanted to follow Jefferies: to settle down and write seriously. Jefferies was the inspirer; and it should be said that he was not like W. H. Hudson. Despite the fact that he wrote the classic *Hodge and his Masters* (1880), Jefferies knew more about fields, rivers, and moorlands than about the habits of villagers.

It was in order to bring dreams to reality, to live out his convictions about artistic values, that Williamson came to Skirr Cottage in the remote village of Georgeham, in Devon. In the years just after the first world war there was much for the artist's eye to see. The traditional life had a culture which had not yet been changed by tourism or the mass media. To get this life into a form editors would accept was difficult and tedious. This would-be writer, too intelligent to believe he could learn quickly a very difficult craft, kept a notebook, observed people, tried to probe the inner lives of a reserved and suspicious group of people.

Even a man with high ideals, concerned with the fraternity of nations, had to get enough to eat, to take thought for the morrow. This he never failed to do. His brain was active and his vitality abounding. So, after memories of the war had drifted back to his consciousness, the autobiographical, self-exploratory faculties started to function. They created an excitement because he didn't want to write fiction, or anything else, that had no relation to his own experience. The search for truth meant contact with people, and he had fortunately met the beautiful and steadfast Loetitia Hibbert; in 1925 they were married in the tiny church perched on an acclivity at Landcross, near Bideford.

Henry on Exmoor, 1960's

Work now loomed up in a way known only to professional writers dependent entirely on the pen for a livelihood. Those who have read a life of Samuel Taylor Coleridge, the novels of George Gissing, or *The Private Papers of Henry Ryecroft*, Gissing's brief account of an author at ease, will have an idea of what this sort of struggle means. This hard literary toil leaves its mark. It also increases the habit of self-absorption, the desire for isolation, and the demand for quietness.

Probably, Williamson's career can be divided into several parts; but his development — for the purpose of this analysis — has two phases, shaped mainly by the wars he knew and the passions, and compassion, they generated. Chronology was not important to the mind of a man who was fated to bear the weight of war-memories all his life. However, the story of Willie Maddison, as told in the novels *The Beautiful Years* (1921), *Dandelion Days* (1922), *The Dream of Fair Women* (1924), and *The Pathway* (1928) constitute the imaginative part of a first phase in his writing life brought together finally in the tetralogy *The Flax of Dream*.

Williamson was not satisfied with the portrayal of Willie Maddison's life. For very many years he saw this as the forerunner of a bigger chronicle. In the same year as *The Pathway* was published, however, another side of this writer's talent was revealed. In 1927 he published *Tarka the Otter*, and a year later he was awarded the Hawthornden Prize. This made his reputation, and with the proceeds he was able to buy a field at Ox's Cross, above his village of Georgeham, where he built his hut, his solitary place which he had dreamed of for a long time.

I think that no matter what critics say to the contrary, *Tarka* will always be associated with Williamson's name, just as the Exmoor romance *Lorna Doone* has blotted out in public esteem the other novels of R. D. Blackmore. To

Henry Williamson with friends: Cannock Chase, 1975

say that *Springhaven* is a better book will not affect the situation at all, as Blackmore found to his chagrin.

There is no evidence, so far as I know, that Henry Williamson regretted *Tarka*'s immense success. What he did fear was that a continuous association of *Tarka* with his name could cause some readers to suppose that he had written only one book. His sensitivity to the environment of his area and his concern for animal life in general gave *Tarka* its power. Sometimes the author's feelings did not coincide with the feelings of local landowners who made up the hunting fraternity. Yet he took endless trouble not to make factual errors, even consulting William Henry Rogers, Esquire, 'late Tutor in college at Eton and sometime Master of the Cheriton Hunt'. He dedicated the book to this oracle; but Williamson's mind could never be confined within parochial limits. Like 'Loony Dick' Jefferies in the area around Coate, in Wiltshire, Henry Williamson knew, as all writers know, that he was an object of occasional derision among those who 'knew' so much that they were unaware of how little they really knew.

At the time of Williamson's funeral, when, ironically, the final scenes of his account of Tarka's life were being filmed on the river Torridge, many accounts about him appeared in newspapers. One eager reporter said: 'More than anyone, Henry Williamson, author of *Tarka the Otter*, who died earlier this year, realised nature to be a spiritual discovery worth pursuing through literature. So concerned was he "to get it just right", he told me, that he re-wrote one book, *Salar the Salmon*, seventeen times and spent five thousand hours watching the fish before he started.'[9]

It is a pity this writer did not 'get it right'. According to Henry's own account *Tarka* was rewritten seventeen times; but the dreaded *Salar* book, the forced successor, written to meet a demand, was written against the clock by a man in constant agony. The author has told us about this reluctance to do the work, and how, to earn the £750 of advanced royalties, he had to sit and type for many hours, sending the sheets direct to the printer without possibility of revision. This book sold three thousand copies in one day, and within about a year the royalties were paid off and the whole episode stored in a memory given to remembering both rights and wrongs.[10]

When *Salar* appeared in 1935 Henry Williamson thought he had sucked dry the imaginative stuff of his own district. He had also realised that his politics weren't popular. He spoke too freely at a time when it would have been better not to have spoken at all. He genuinely believed that he was an uncomplicated man who also could play the role of prophet. These were mistakes.

Williamson has written about his working aims and about his criterion as to what was true or false: 'The nearer I can get to the labourer, the artisan, the decent professional man, the good working squire, the happier and more secure I feel. My ideal, my hope, is to be able to work and to live so that I may serve the English people by making coherent their inner *geist* or aspirations, and so accelerate the making of the nation into one large family. Natural man on his natural earth: the highest philosophical truth.'[11]

This is close to the 'mud and mysticism' school fostered by those who knew little about work on the land, such as Rolf Gardiner, Lady Eve Balfour, Lord Portsmouth, and many more; although, so far as I know, Williamson had no connection with the Springhead Ring or The Soil Association. This was a wholly subjective reaction, because Williamson was an observer; although he learned much about manual work. He lacked the direct knowledge of a novelist like Stephen Reynolds, author of *A Poor Man's House*, who was in immediate touch with cottage life because he lived with the fishermen Bob and Tom Woolley of Sidmouth.

Care has to be shown in evaluating any work by Williamson, because he had the skill and commitment of a true artist. Two works of his which are not mentioned often enough, *Tales of a Devon Village* and *Life in a Devon Village*, were published in 1945. In a preface to the former work he wrote: '*Tales of a Devon Village*, with its companion volume *Life in a Devon Village*, is compiled with material gathered together originally in two books I wrote between 1919 and 1929 and called *The Village Book* and *The Labouring Life*. Both dealt with an observed and authenticated period that has now passed away—the first decade of the interval between the two industrial wars of the twentieth century. I was never fully satisfied by them; they were a collection of varying fragments rather than unified books.'

This search for unity, the feeling that earlier writing was a betrayal of the self, characterised all Williamson's musings on his work. He was insecure in the way that Edward Thomas was insecure, fighting for something he could see in the far distance. One is forced to accept the fact that Williamson is precisely as the thoughtful writer Colin Wilson described him: 'a very complex bag of tricks'.[12]

The self-denigration, something close to his creative faculty early and late, does not cancel out the fact that much of what he wrote about his own region has a stylistic beauty of enviable distinction. The self-consciously mannered Dorset essayist Llewelyn Powys, for all his aping of Lamb and Pater, can never match Henry at his lyrical best. I find myself continually discovering new facets of this man; seeing how indisputable is his stature as a writer.

Very early in his career (and very late) he was vibrant with life, eager to communicate, and to make love to young women. The child in him never died, as was true of Walter de la Mare, W. H. Davies, and J. M. Barrie. In the first phase of his writing life, even if he felt himself to be an explorer, he let us come close to his hearth and home. No one should forget *The Children of Shallowford*, *The Sun in the Sands*, or *Goodbye West Country* in the search for the man behind the smokestream.

He tried to come close to Devon life, and to Devon people like 'Stroyle' George, or 'Sparker' Ley, or 'The Zeale Brothers'—and with a lot of success. Perhaps his dialogue outshines his use of dialect, of which he did not always show a mastery. He did certainly listen carefully when old people spoke the dialect, and some of his critics knew far less about dialectal inflections than he did. I'm sure it is an exaggeration to argue that Williamson deliberately fathered 'fake words' on the Devon dialect, as one Exmoor man claimed. This elicited a comment at the end of *Tarka*, which should be noted.[13]

I would be willing to admit that some of the words he uses seem strange to me. For instance, I am put off by the use of the expression '*Noomye*'. I've recorded the memories of aged people in most parts of the country, and this expression was not known to them. They brushed it aside with a confident reliance on their own long years of acquaintance with a form of speech now disappearing, except in isolated districts. Did Williamson strive for literary effect, or were there people who did use this sort of exclamation?

One word which I do not know, but which I am sure Henry Williamson did know, is 'Ackymals' (for tomtits), about which he has written in his portrayal of John Kift and other Georgeham folk, who are able to recognise themselves, according to a member of the well-known Gammon family when he spoke to me ten or twelve years ago.

In his defence, written in 1927, against the charge of foisting fake words on the Devon dialect in *Tarka*, this visionary was looking forward to our featureless future, to the time when the landscape of power was to be invested by planners, engineers, and hordes of exploiters with an ugly uniformity, a legacy of the technology that everyone needs and no one wants. Along with tourists, weekenders, and newcomers, other seekers after urbanism are ceaselessly at work felling the trees, ripping into vast acres of agricultural land, and destroying the old and the beautiful in favour of their monstrous sacrifices to Moloch.

'Another reason for using local words and phrases', wrote Williamson more than forty years ago, 'was to preserve them before they passed away. The daily newspapers, now beginning to reach remote villages, are making a stereotyped speech in rural England; wireless will further a uniform pronunciation. Today even middle-aged men are inclined to be a little shy of their natural speech, sometimes apologising for it when talking with visitors in the street or pub . . .'

Williamson himself was the privileged spectator who was not anxious to see the ordinary folk get the amenities he had enjoyed. Hardy in one of his essays opposed such a notion, saying that progress and picturesqueness did not harmonise. No matter how skilled he might be, the inquiring writer can't get close to traditional speech in a closed society. Williamson was uncertain in his rendering of the ancient farming rhyme — applied to farms all over Devon — and especially where the farmers were known to be 'near'; that is, neither to pay well, eat well, or keep themselves or their visitors warm. It was the comment of the collective, the extended family, on the lives of some working farmers so mean in the matter of payment that their own sons had low wages and could not afford to marry until they had reached middle age. This was the band of brethren who found it hard to acquire money and impossible to spend it.

Over to Pickerswell
'Mongst the trees
Barley bread
And vinned cheese
Reasty bacon
Tough as thong
Darned if I stop
There very long.

In this 'Ploughboy's Chant' he writes 'vinned' cheese and 'reasty' bacon, and follows this with 'tough as thong'. In the many renderings I have recorded the words are rendered in a slightly different way: 'Vinneid' cheese, 'risty' bacon, and 'tough's a thong'. This is the side of the early Williamson not uncharacteristic of a hasty novelist in the early stages of his career. He was accused by T. E. Lawrence's somewhat tetchy brother of not having a scholar's eye. This man didn't know that there was no time for exact scholarship. There was money to be earned, a wife and child to support.

Yet when Williamson looked at Ham of an evening and heard church bells sounding across valley and moorland like tinkling glass, he felt a sense of oneness. He knew that his locality, his described universe, was one enshrining the good and evil of the world. The gentry, the farmers, military and civil authority, meant much to an officer with certain standards to observe. In addition there was the clash of values, the struggle of nations and classes, not absent even from the peace of Ham. When shadows darkened over Westminster and the night began to close in on the chronicler of Ox's Cross, he glimpsed something of what the world faced. With his mystical traits, the strange forces within himself, Williamson could get close to the essence of the modern dilemma in a time when too many sought wealth, power, and domination.

'The village is as the nation, as the continent, as the

world', he wrote in *Tales of a Devon Village*. This was a lesson historians learned slowly; but it was learned. There was a need not only to narrate and reconstruct, but also to interpret. History had to do with thought, with ideas that made the events and created the environment.

The man who bought the field at Ox's Cross did not sell it. He did begin to think he would move away; take refuge on the land as a farmer, using strength of body to bring back vitality to a tired mind and a tortured spirit. It was then, in 1937, that he published the book of jottings, the scrapbook, or commonplace book, that remains one of my favourites: *Goodbye West Country*. It gave forth an ominous sound to herald in a period of danger and death.

IN AN ESSAY on the work of Henry Williamson, John Middleton Murry, the critic and former editor of *The Adelphi*, suggested that the natural history books, the 'country' books and the autobiographical works, were no more than the by-products of a mind intensely pre-occupied with big imaginative tasks.[14] I am not sure that this is true. During the twenty years from the publication of *The Pathway* in 1928 to the appearance of that suggestive and symbolic novel *The Phasian Bird* in 1948 much had happened to Williamson.

What his situation was in 1937 we know because the book he published in that year was a declaration and a cry from the heart. Williamson was always a contradiction, in the way that D. H. Lawrence and the more devious T. E. Lawrence were contradictions. He believed that at this point one phase of his life was ending. It is essential to see how the Williamson who felt that his past was unfulfilled compared with the man determined to be a dispassionate artist viewing his age with the eye of one who would look outward and be prepared to accept the scarrings of social life with a quiet irony.

The ambivalence in Henry Williamson's nature could

be illustrated in many ways. One that has concerned me was brought into the open when I happened to read his pamphlet *The Wild Red Deer of Exmoor*, published as far back as 1931. I read it more than twenty years later and found it at times disconcerting. Some people asked Williamson about his attitude to various forms of hunting, and his replies were evasions. This digression on what he called the logic, ethics, and economics of staghunting was meant to be a commentary on life around Exmoor. When he went to an anti-staghunting gathering in the town hall at Lynton, he tried to be impartial, desiring to see both sides of the argument.

He was covertly on the side of the sportsman; but this could have been brought about because he had to live in a place like Georgeham and maintain the illusion that he held views similar to the average inhabitant of the place. Which he did not. Much more serious for the man of thought and action, the novelist, naturalist, and soldier was the threat of a second world war. He had said that his standards had not reached the heights his mind had envisaged. He also remembered the ingratitude of villagers, and reacted about what he thought was a non-existent 'village mind'. That mind remembered him on the day he was buried in the churchyard at Georgeham. He felt himself lost 'in the ancient sunlight of the past'. As he says in his book of farewell, it seemed as though his work was finished.

He had written all he could write about otter, salmon, stag, villages, and moorland. All those memories and hopes were temporarily buried in the ancient sunlight of the place that was home. Now he would leave them. That was the past, and for him, as an artist, all life was the past. For those reasons he bought a derelict farm in Norfolk. The story of Old Hall Farm is told in his book *The Story of a Norfolk Farm*.

There were many other reasons dormant in his mind

when he moved from a place he knew and understood to
one he did not know and would not want to understand.
Also, by this time his sympathy for Sir Oswald Mosley and
the British Union of Fascists had become generally known
in Devon. When war started he was for a very brief time
imprisoned under Regulation 18B of the Defence of the
Realm Act. Some had thought he was an undesirable person. He became an object of official and local suspicion.
People even searched his dustbins to discover anything
that would incriminate the 'spy'. It was the sort of treatment meted out to D. H. Lawrence, who turned around
and snapped in his usual fashion at the 'Cornish asses,
apes, and dogs'.

As I have already inferred, much of the criticism was
quite out of focus. Williamson's political leanings were
authoritarian, but he had been a soldier. More than that,
he was an admirer of the 'heroes', the men slightly larger
than life who courted publicity and wanted to control the
destiny of their country. Happily for everyone they failed.

Those who look more deeply into Williamson's mind
will see clear evidence of a purpose. When war was almost
a certainty he wanted his hero T. E. Lawrence to visit
Hitler and work some kind of miracle. The dreams in his
mind had not died away. They were preserved in the
ancient sunlight of the first world war. No doubt
Williamson himself had thought of acting out a special
peacemaking role, as ascribed to Phillip Maddison in *The
Phoenix Generation*. Did he not possess a special clarity
derived from the essence of all things, and conferred on
the artist as on the mystic?

'Will not this immediately be recognised if I go, my
unafraid self, in the name and spirit of the *camaraderie*,
with all the hopes of the dead and living of the Western
Front on Christmas Day, 1914?'[15]

It was the question of a mind *in extremis*, of a spirit
that had long before lost hold on political realities.

DURING THOSE YEARS 1937 to 1945 Williamson wrote over a million words: 'It was a punishing, also cathartic time. The worst part of it was the feeling of failure, of guilt that one had fallen so far beneath the standards that one knew to be right. I was permanently tired, sleepless, often bitter, generally without hope, seeing myself as a microcosm of a Europe in travail.'

In his study of Williamson's novels Middleton Murry does not underestimate the value of the big task generically entitled *A Chronicle of Ancient Sunlight*. He does tend to think that there was a gulf between the Williamson who wrote *The Flax of Dream* (the Willie Maddison tetralogy), and the man who was destined in 1948 to begin his series of novels about Phillip Maddison. I take the view that Henry Williamson's work as a novelist, autobiographer, and naturalist is all of a piece. When he returned from Norfolk to his field and his village he began what must have been a conscious process of artistic redemption.

All that had gone before was a preparation for this new beginning. Or this was his view, resulting from an underestimation of earlier work. At this stage comparison between the two sagas would be fruitless and premature. The pattern evolved in the Phillip Maddison saga I know in some detail. In the harsh winter of 1963, when snow was piled high in lanes and fields, Henry Williamson visited me to talk about himself and the problems associated with his massive project. He was trying to bring his long chronicle to an end. He passed to me a long tin box containing many typescripts, rewrites of novels that were to be the concluding volumes of the Chronicle.

He had previously sought the guidance of other friends who were also professional writers: Middleton Murry, Malcolm Elwin, and Sir John Heygate, who lived in Ireland and was known to me only as a novelist. Murry had been extremely circumspect on what to include, but

had said that it would not be very wise for Williamson to
parade his sympathies for the British Union of Fascists.
Elwin was reader for the firm publishing the *Chronicle*,
and I am sure his advice was on similar lines.

The problem was that Henry could not make up his
mind about what to *exclude*. I worked on this for some
weeks, and finally drew up a kind of index suggesting
sections that seemed unlikely to advance the narrative.
He acted on some of these points. I did suggest that at no
time should he use the swastika as a symbol or dedicate
any book to the Mosleys. Both these suggestions he dis-
regarded.[16] This was a mistake, because sales suffered;
many admirers of Williamson's work felt that they had
been misled and rebuffed. They made known the fact
that 'the public' found nothing amusing in his antics.

I would not want to overstate the case against Sir
Oswald Mosley, much as I deplore his views. As Richard
Crossman said, he had the temperament and all the at-
tributes of a professional politician. But he lacked
humility; and so Williamson, following at a great
distance, was dazzled because his political and social
understanding was as limited as that of P. G. Wodehouse. This is not difficult to understand, because his
mind had been totally exercised in other directions.

My opinion, after long talks with Williamson over the
years, is that this writer's mind was not released from the
traumatic experience of trench warfare which he had
endured as a youth. This frozen mind, chilled at the
thought of war, somehow wished to make reparation, to
find excuses for German belligerence, even for the
raucous fanaticism of Hitler.

It is vital for Williamson's sake to remember this: *his
purpose at the beginning and to the end was humani-
tarian, not political.*

The pattern of Phillip Maddison's life, followed with so
much detail over so long a period, might not be, is not,

identical with that of Williamson, although there are basic resemblances. Like Parson Hawker of Morwenstow before him, this Puck or Peter Pan did not always know where to draw the line between fact and fancy. He loved to embroider ideas, to turn the ordinary garden flower into an orchid. The creation of beauty was his business.

This man's mind and effort — so deserving of public recognition — was denied it because he somehow could not see the errors in peculiar and persistent political allegiance. None of us can see the whole truth. His creed was from the heart, and he was outside the arena of serious political debate.

Middleton Murry was fair and just to Williamson when he brought into the open what could not be concealed. He states the matter fairly; I can't envisage any of Henry's friends thinking otherwise:

What in this perspective is the adolescent enthusiasm for Adolf Hitler, in which Mr Williamson began at this time to indulge? It is the vicarious justification of a philosophy of life, a theory of the causation of war, which Mr Williamson knows in his inward being, from his daily experience, to be either false or completely hopeless.

Sadly, it was both; and did Phillip Maddison (or Williamson his creator) get any closer to the truth, to an admission of Hitler's demonic folly and of the errors of those who were his friends in Britain? Time alone can answer that question. There is much yet to be learned about the Anglo-German Bund and about the identities of people lurking behind the scenes of history. What is quite certain, I think, is that the creator of *Tarka*, like it or not, will always be remembered as long as books about animals are read; and no student of Henry Williamson's work and mental constitution should ever forget the wise words of his American publisher, which make a fitting end to this brief commentary:

You are so many kinds of a man that it is almost impossible for those who care for you to comprehend you. But after you have lived this life in Norfolk, one of these days you will write a book by a new Henry Williamson. I predict for the new book a success, provided you are able to subdue that strange and unmanageable self who has so often slapped you in your own face.

Henry Williamson wrote not one book but many in reparation. The question for future readers to answer is this: Did he subdue a side of his personality, thus hiding the real man from our sight? and will the *Chronicle*, like *Tarka* and *Salar*, be symbolic of Williamson's personality for ever? Perhaps time will lend its magnanimity to genius, and there will be light over Taw and Torridge, over Georgeham, Barnstaple, and Braunton, and over the graves of 'Stroyle' George, the Zeale brothers, and the Gammons, who lie now in the churchyard at Georgeham where Henry Williamson was buried on 18 August 1977.

NOTES

1. *The New Anglo-Saxon Pamphlets*, edited by John Atkins, 1944.
2. G. Cavaliero, *The Rural Tradition in the English Novel, 1900-1939*: (Macmillan, 1977), p.188.
3. V. S. Pritchett, in *Why Do I Write?* (Percival Marshall, 1948), p.7.
4. *New Writing in Europe* (Pelican Books, 1940), pp.16-17.
5. Sir Victor Pritchett: born 1900.
6. George Orwell, 'In Defence of P. G. Wodehouse', in *Critical Essays* (Secker and Warburg, 1946).
7. In *Gangrel*, edited by J. B. Pick (Leicester, n.d.), p.7.
8. Ibid.
9. 'Smile on the Face of the Otter', *The Sunday Times*, 1 December 1977.

10. Cf. Henry Williamson, 'A Personal Note', in *The Henry Williamson Animal Saga* (Macdonald, 1960), pp.372-375.
11. Henry Williamson, *Goodbye West Country* (Putnam, 1937), p.313.
12. Colin Wilson, 'Henry Williamson', in *The Aylesford Review*, vol. 4, no. 4, 1961.
13. Letter to *The London Mercury*, February 1928, reprinted, with short commentary, under the heading 'Apologia pro verbis meis', in *The Henry Williamson Animal Saga*, pp.196-199.
14. John Middleton Murry, 'The Novels of Henry Williamson', a sixty-five page essay in *Katherine Mansfield and Other Literary Studies* (Constable, 1959).
15. Henry Williamson, *The Phoenix Generation* (Macdonald, 1965), p.379.
16. The Royal Air Force roundel and the Luftwaffe's swastika appear on the spine of the dust-jacket of the Macdonald edition of *The Phoenix Generation*, and the front of the dust-jacket bears symbolic adaptations of the Union Jack and the flag of National Socialist Germany.

'THE FLAX OF DREAM'

David Hoyle

FOR MOST READERS, and certainly for most of the critics who have cared to look at his work, Henry Williamson is predominantly a nature writer. Volumes of nature and animal stories, countless articles about rural life, and of course *Tarka the Otter* and its variants, have all formed and confirmed this impression. So too have the early novels which collectively comprise *The Flax of Dream*, telling as they do the story of one man's growth in a rural environment to a naturally-conditioned philosophy which seems to challenge the ideas of society. The fifth volume of this sequence, *The Star-Born*, is offered to us as a distillation of that philosophy, a 'Gospel' (as Williamson called it) for the modern world. Unfortunately for his literary reputation, that philosophy does not really bear close examination, nor do the novels which outline it have a great deal of claim to serious literary attention. Had they been all that Williamson had written, the almost unanimous decision of academic and professional critics to ignore him might have been justified: and yet it would be impossible fully to weigh or understand the achievement of those seven good novels which Williamson did write later in his career, and which make up the first half of his *Chronicle of Ancient Sunlight*, without looking back to the literary and personal influences which helped shape *The Flax of Dream*. Such influences, especially those which arose from the conditions of his early family life, were responsible both for the attempts at evasion which characterise Williamson's early writings, and, paradoxically, for the fictional structures and devices which he had later to evolve to control that evasion. Once the evolution had taken place — and it was to take Williamson longer than almost any modern author to achieve it — the limitations apparent in his early writings were strikingly overcome. Indeed, it is almost true to say that the creative tensions which lend the later novels their dynamism are tensions between the wish for an escape from, and the need for an understanding of, reality; or between the desire for 'dream' and the duty to chronicle, as honestly as possible, the factors which make up self. Constantly in Williamson's mature fiction, even at its very best, one can detect the tendency to evade or explain away certain realities, to handle characters in ways which are less than honest, or which fail to explore their full identities and responsibilities; often, one feels authorial attempts to excuse self, to shift blame onto environment or history. Happily, those tendencies are generally held in check by a style of fiction which refuses to allow simplifications, and which forces moral decisions back to areas of personal guilt or innocence presented through characters responsible, as individuals, for their own actions. All this activates Williamson's later work at its best, and to understand its origins it is necessary to understand *The Flax of Dream* not as the inspired message of a modern nature-prophet (exactly the function Williamson wished for it), but as an ultimately mistaken attempt to escape from a difficult self.

Before looking at the factors which produced *The Flax* it may be as well briefly to remind ourselves of what happens in these four novels. We begin, in *The Beautiful Years* (1921) with a childhood that is in many ways ideal, in that it is set in what Williamson was later to describe as 'a far, imagined countryside, with imagined characters derived from memories of . . . boyhood'. In the same passage from *The Innocent Moon* (one of the *Chronicle* novels), Williamson confesses that this writing is 'an escape from real life', an evasion of the complexities which beset him in the deracinated years immediately after the Great War. Indeed, apart from a few darker moments, the tone of this first novel is well enough characterised by the quotation from Richard Jefferies with which Williamson prefaces it: 'The sun shone there for a very long time, and the water rippled and sang.' In the sepia-coloured light cast by that sun, an imaginary nostalgia re-enacts the nature-idyll which, by his own confession, Williamson was denied in his own suburban childhood. Similarly, in the next novel, *Dandelion Days* (1922), little happens in terms of plot or event, and the emphasis falls upon the attempts to create a rural paradise in which youth and nature are brought into happy contact. The period of this second novel is separated from that of the third, *The Dream of Fair Women* (1924), by the 1914-18 war, in which its hero, Willie Maddison, is involved. When we recommence the tale in 1919, however, the war exists only in the background. References are made to it and to its effects upon the characters' minds, but all direct re-creations are avoided. Instead, the fiction centres upon Willie Maddison's unsatisfactory love-affair with a sophisticated woman in Folkestone; an affair which ends as the novel does, prompting Willie to return to Devon and a life as a nature-solitary. There we find him in the last novel, *The Pathway* (1928), except that his intended solitude is spoiled by another affair, this time with a far more sympathetic woman. However, by now Maddison's belief in the power of nature has begun seriously to displace him in his own society; spurned by most of those he wishes to convert, and eventually finding even his fiancée confused by his ideas, he is accidentally drowned at the climax and conclusion of the book. Only then is his true worth recognised by those around him, so that the drowning is presented very much as an apotheosis which bears a real message for our own unregenerate world.

These things, briefly, are the salient events in the tetralogy. If we looked for many developed characters, for explorations of complex relationships or for a truly consequential plot, we should be disappointed. The concentration is upon atmosphere — the atmosphere of a dream — and upon the emerging philosophy of 'natural truth'. That combination has its origins in two kinds of influence, literary and personal; both go far towards explaining the nature of *The Flax of Dream*, and its failure as a work of fiction. They also have much to tell us about Williamson.

We can trace the ideas underlying *The Flax* back to Wordsworth's *Prelude* of 1805, and more generally to the Romantic belief that an understanding of the child provides an understanding of the adult into which it grows. And yet Williamson did not return to or assimilate the really fundamental discoveries made here by his Romantic predecessors. Rather than look at the ways in which Wordsworth used a re-creation of the 'fair seed time' as a means to knowledge of his adult self, Williamson seems to have focused instead upon a quite strange version of the original process. It is not to Rousseau, Blake, Wordsworth, George Eliot, or Charlotte Brontë that he looked for ideas about fiction dealing with children, but to Francis Thompson and Richard Jefferies; worthy writers both, in their own limited ways, but certainly not men able to revivify, add to, or even fully interpret the traditions in which they were writing. The influence of Jefferies's *Bevis* is obvious. It is a pleasant enough book, but it is essentially a children's novel, an extended reverie into a peaceful adventure world where a child is untroubled by any hint of its coming adult self. But it is not only to *Bevis* that Williamson looked for a model: Jefferies's last work, *The Story of My Heart*, also provides him with much that underlies *The Flax*. The main task of Jefferies's *Story* is to explain a type of nature-mysticism

experienced by the author; a transcendence of ordinary
life through a deep concentration upon natural beauty.
The seminal passage is one in which he describes such a
moment, achieved after a climb to the summit of the
Wiltshire Downs. That climb, and some of its effects,
have a provenance going back to Wordsworth's 'Ascent of
Snowdon' in Book XIII of *The Prelude*. Certainly,
Williamson himself reproduces Jefferies's experience on
numerous occasions throughout *The Flax*. In each of
them we can detect the specific influence: the settings, on
sunlit downs amid thyme and birdsong, are all the same;
the results, of brief transcendence into another realm,
very similar. If we were to relate Willie Maddison's experiences back to Wordsworth's, we should find a significant departure. It is more than simply the difference
between Wordsworth's perception of a Romantically
sublime beauty and Williamson's of a pleasantly abstract,
sunlit one. The difference lies rather in the sense the
reader feels, in Wordsworth's version, of a real autobiographical experience, immediate and threateningly
powerful. Wordsworth's prototypical vision leads to
speculation and intellectual theory, rather than to the
brief escapes enjoyed by his successors. This comparison
is important not because it makes the obvious point that
Wordsworth is a 'better' writer than Williamson, but to
remind ourselves that in one narrow sense they share a
common tradition, and to explain that Williamson's
intentions for *The Flax of Dream* as a revolutionary work,
as the first expression of the powers of nature, were fun-
damentally mistaken. This is how he expressed the idea
on one occasion:

How could the new way of life be brought into the minds of
millions of people? . . . This new world could only come from
early contacts with Nature; the pure thoughts given by the
elements must be the philosophical basis of the new world.[1]

And this, even more revealingly, is how he conceived of the effect of this 'message' upon himself and his fiction:

Very secretly within myself I thought that evolution had, in me, chosen to take a leap forward: that the ideas which burned in me had never been expressed in the world before.[2]

In 1939, ten years after the completion of *The Flax*, Williamson seemed still to maintain this conviction: he wrote then that

one day the idea that burned in [his] brain would be made real, that [he] was the prophet of a new order, a new world.[3]

Perhaps we may smile at this self-deception; but to understand it, and the ideas underlying *The Flax of Dream*, we need to look back to another of the writings which influenced the novel sequence, and also at the personal circumstances which helped shape it. Francis Thompson's essay 'Shelley' underlies much of Williamson's writing, early and late; but nowhere does he take it so seriously as in these four novels. In his essay Thompson seeks to define the factors which produced the poetic sensibilities of his subject. However, one cannot help feeling that it was written — and was used by Williamson — to justify his own isolation and social difficulties, rather than with any clear eye on the ideologically or linguistically vigorous aspects of Shelley's writing. What Thompson explains, if anything, is the possible origin of one idea of Shelley; the weak, life-avoiding side. What he cannot account for, of course, are the particular springs of his genius: yet those are what he appears to explain. His ideas are fairly summarised in passages like these:

[Shelley, as a child] threw out a reserve, encysted in which he grew to maturity unaffected by the intercourses that modify the maturity of others into [manhood] . . . Most poets . . . are prepared for their mission by an initial segregation, as the seed is buried to germinate: before they can utter the oracle of poetry, they must first be divided from the body of men.

We need only consider for a second the 'most poets' here to understand how generally wrong Thompson is. Chaucer, Shakespeare, Donne, Byron, and, one suspects, Shelley himself for much of the time, were living, active men; their poetry a product of both thought and intense, varied human experiences. We can understand how Thompson may have wished to promote this view of poets: if Shelley were a lonely, isolated man and also a great poet, might it not follow that another such isolated man could also be a poet? Williamson did not question Thompson's theory, nor wonder what personal factors may have conditioned it. Instead, he has tried to reproduce Thompson's ideas in his own fiction, and also in his own conception of himself. Jim Holloman, the solitary, misunderstood co-hero of *The Beautiful Years*, a man with a mystical appreciation of nature, represents one version of the Thompson model; Willie Maddison himself, Williamson's *soisi*, is obviously another. Both men are isolated, both childlike, both are supposed to utter the oracle of poetry; in Jim's case it is a barely articulated joy-in-nature, in Willie's a sadly misunderstood philosophy of 'natural' revolution against the evils of industrialism. The following passage from *The Beautiful Years* is a revealing one. In it, the aegis of nature-mysticism is passed on from Jim (who, it should be added, bears close physical and ideological resemblances to Richard Jefferies) to the nine-year-old Willie. The prose of this passage, as of many others in the four novels, reveals a great deal about the influences of literature upon Williamson, and about his attitude to nature in his early writings. Willie, who has run away from home, has passed the night in Jim's hut. At dawn, they both awake:

Over the dark outline of the beech wood hung a star, a lustrous globe of radiance . . . They watched it in silence. Slowly it moved higher, glowing with softer and purer blaze as it was lapped by the light now flowing into the eastern estuary of heaven . . . The darkness paled before the spectral dawn . . . light, mystic light, the life of the world, was flooding like an incoming tide into the dusked shallows of the dawn . . . A thrush flung clear notes from an oak outstanding in the covert . . . One by one the stars in deeper heaven grew wan and sunk into the waters of the day. Like a motionless sea, light swept up the sky, purging it of darkness, glowing in the lofty empyrean . . . [Willie] determined to be a moucher, like Jim, when he grew up.

This passage is the departure point for Willie; after this, we are told, nature has claimed him for its own, and his isolation from ordinary human society has begun. Yet the strain which is so apparent in this prose is a strong symptom of the difficulty Williamson has experienced in presenting that crucial divergence. First of all, it is a distinctly 'literary' approach to nature, and literary in a way that distorts its intended sense. Phrases like 'lustrous globe of radiance', 'motionless light' (which nevertheless 'swept'), or 'glowing in the lofty empyrean', all tell clearly of an attempt to intensify the experience by intensifying the language conveying it. The lapse into 'high-style' confirms what one suspects of the book as a whole, that it is based not upon actual experience, but upon fantasy fed by literature. What writer, recalling or re-creating an intensely felt experience of a real dawn, would wish to use the ponderous and distracting sea simile as Williamson does throughout, or fail to separate the descriptions of the morning star and the rising sun? One feels that even if Williamson had been able to describe the event in a way that convinced us of its effects upon the child, the basic idea underlying the change in his life would still be very suspect.

Again, Wordsworth provides us with a useful touch-
stone: if we look in *The Prelude* for any similar attempt
to encapsulate in a single moment 'the growth of a poet's
mind' we would be disappointed. Accumulated hours of
feeling and experience are analysed for us, and the links
between them delicately and exploringly analysed.
Huckleberry Finn, too, tells of the effects of non-human
life upon a boy, and suggests a similar divergence from
ordinary society as a result. But, again, the language, like
the process, is relaxed and naturalistic; the change is left
for the boy to feel and explain as best he can. As a result,
we can believe what happens as Huck and Tom drift
downstream into a new understanding:

We catched fish, and talked, and took a swim now and then to
keep off sleepiness. It was kind of solemn, drifting down the big
still river, laying on our backs looking up at the stars, and we
didn't ever feel like talking.

Again, this contrast between an effective 'kind of solemn'
and a diverting 'lustrous globe of radiance' is suggested,
not to remind ourselves that Williamson at this stage of
his career was a less capable writer than Mark Twain or
Wordsworth, but to focus on the particular problems of
the novel sequence. The scene with Holloman is crucial,
for it is implicitly – and sometimes explicitly – intended
as the rationale of all that subsequently happens. All of
Willie's 'strange' ideas, all of his difficulties and his
eventual death, are to be traced back to this moment of
segregation. Because this moment, and many others like
it, can be seen to rest not upon real or truthfully imagined experience of nature, but upon an *idea* of nature
and a self-conscious interpretation of it, then the subsequent philosophy is exposed as false. In *The Star-Born*,
a 'mystical' work appended to *The Flax*, the same process
of initiation into nature is repeated exactly, and again the

feeling one derives is of an intention, a semi-literary idea, being pushed at the reader without exploration, qualification or question. As long as we are prepared to accept that nature is 'better' than nurture, that non-human society inculcates truths superior to those of men and women, or that we have lost more than we have gained since the Industrial Revolution, then *The Flax*'s ideas may seem viable. If, however, we question those ideas, or wish to look to other writers, like Lawrence, for a detailed exposition of some of their origins in twentieth-century thought, then we cannot but be dissatisfied with *The Flax of Dream*.

What, then, apart from these literary influences, conditioned Williamson's choice of such ideas? The revealing sentence from *The Innocent Moon* gives us a key: *The Flax* is, above all, an 'escape from real life'. The titles themselves suggest it; it is a *dream*, whether of an idyllic rural boyhood, of fair women, or of a road to posthumous recognition as a seer. All of Williamson's autobiographical writings attest to this. Disorganised as *The Innocent Moon* and *It Was the Nightingale* are, they are at least more honest in their presentation of Williamson's post-war years than the early novels. In those later books the attempts at self-romanticism can still be found; so too can the desire to escape into fantasy; but interwoven with them is a strong sense of personal defeat and deracination after the war. By relating those things back to the period from 1920 to 1928, when *The Flax* was being written, we can see more clearly how the attempts to concoct a 'philosophy' of natural truth, and to establish himself as a modern seer, may well have been no more than a means of evading the difficult rebuilding of self that was really necessary, and which was to come much later in Williamson's life.

All of this will have seemed strangely negative, and yet it is an essential part of my own respect for Williamson's

later writing to be quite clear about what he had to overcome in order to achieve it. It is not only that dangerous
tendencies to self-deceit and self-aggrandisement are
revealed in these early novels, but that the means of over-
coming those tendencies are integral parts of what the
later fiction *discovers*. There is not space here for me to
go into details about those discoveries, and such ground
is, anyway, being covered elsewhere. However, I would
like to suggest that comparisons between *The Flax of
Dream* and the first three novels of the *Chronicle of
Ancient Sunlight*, and then again between this early
tetralogy and the best novels dealing with the Great War
(*How Dear is Life*, *The Golden Virgin*, and *Love and the
Loveless*) reveal a width of development quite un-
paralleled in modern fiction. If in these early works
Williamson is concerned with self-evasion, with a retreat
into a fantasy world, and with a literary tradition he has
failed to question, we must not be misled, as most critics
have been, into thinking that such things are the limits of
his powers. In *Young Phillip Maddison*, for example, we
will find a description of a childhood handled in ways
which bear practically no relationship with the early
novels. In the later work the idyll has been changed for a
painfully realistic exploration of a troubled childhood; an
exploration which reaches out to question the effect of
parents' aberrant sexuality upon their children; which
forces us to define the intricate relationships between
event, character and environment; and which then goes
on, in subsequent volumes of the series, to feed this
material into our own whole conception of character.
There are, of course, residual attempts to suggest that
nature is the salve for all human ills, but these are made
to seem merely superficial in term of the fiction's overall
complexity and vitality. It is hard for us to imagine what
kinds of mental processes were involved in Williamson's
development from *The Flax* to the *Chronicle*, although

the key to them seems to lie in the subjects with which the later sequence commences. The coming-to-terms with difficult parents, with a difficult earlier self and with a troubled childhood are all the implicit themes of these first novels of the *Chronicle*. Lawrence's idea, used of *Sons and Lovers*, that 'one sheds one's sicknesses in books, repeats and presents again one's emotions, to be master of them', may well be relevant here. Often, Williamson had confessed that he wished to write of the Great War; instead of beginning with 1914, however, he began with the story of his parents' marriage, and with a childhood recognisably his own. Everything in the novels dealing with the years before 1914, that is, the first three novels of the *Chronicle*, suggests that an abreactive process was taking place, and that the old difficulties inherited from childhood were being worked out, or shed, in Lawrence's terms. Once that shedding had taken place, the significant fiction dealing with the war could be written; before it, in novels like those of *The Flax of Dream*, the problems which haunted Williamson were too severe to be either approached or circumvented. *The Flax of Dream* provides us with an idea of those problems, and of the easy way out of them which Williamson at first chose; by seeing that early sequence as the prelude to a deep struggle and a weighty achievement, and also as a measure of the great distance he had to travel in his writing life, we can have a clearer idea of his courage both as man and writer.

NOTES

1. Henry Williamson, 'Quest', in *Woman's Illustrated*, 13 April 1946.
2. *The Sun in the Sands* (London, 1945), pp.19-20.
3. *The Children of Shallowford* (London, 1939), p.35.

HENRY WILLIAMSON AND *A CHRONICLE OF ANCIENT SUNLIGHT*: AN APPRECIATION

Roger Mortimore

> The work in progress becomes the poet's fate and determines his development. It is not Goethe who creates Faust, but Faust who creates Goethe. (*Jung*)

GEORGE STEINER has stated that *Wolf Solent* by John Cowper Powys is 'the one English novel to rival Tolstoy'. Some might claim this position for Henry Williamson's fifteen-volume sequence. The neglect of *A Chronicle of Ancient Sunlight* raises serious questions about the authenticity of English intellectual life. Williamson's epic is in part a novel of ideas. Was Colin Wilson correct when he wrote that 'the English loathe ideas'? Until recently George Painter was virtually the only distinguished critic to have given due attention to Williamson's novel. This neglect is partly for political reasons. I once saw a public library copy of *A Solitary War* with NAZI BASTARD scrawled across the dedication 'To Oswald and Diana Mosley, in friendship'. Certainly a discussion of the political issues Williamson raises in the novel is necessary. It is also overdue. To understand Williamson's epic the reader must shed his prejudices as Phillip Maddison, the 'passionate pilgrim' of our age, sheds his illusions.

Williamson stated that Phillip Maddison was himself.[1] Apart from the concluding *The Gale of the World*, the novel is mainly an accurate record, based on childhood memories or on journals. Williamson began to journalise during the 1914-1918 war. It has to be admitted that the use of journal material is equivocal. The most vivid parts of the sequence are Phillip's first experience of war in *How Dear Is Life*, and the death of Barley, his first wife, in *It Was The Nightingale*. The battle scenes in Flanders in 1914 are the recalled sensations of a boy of eighteen. Their horror is such as to compel a continual temporary laying-aside of the book. Phillip's marriage to Barley is a fiction. Their brief life together and her death in childbirth have a force of imaginative truth sometimes absent from passages that are a recasting of journal material. The advantage of the journals, of course, is the gain in veracity, in the rightness of the myriad details of daily life. The disadvantage, a serious one, is a tendency to reiteration. Copious extracts from the journal of Phillip Maddison often add nothing new. Certainly this is no worse than the reiteration in some of D. H. Lawrence's work. And the lengthy journal sections do add to the quiddity of Phillip Maddison. They aid an understanding of the dilemmas of our age's 'passionate pilgrim'.

The opening volume, *The Dark Lantern*, deals with the courtship and marriage of Phillip's parents, and Phillip's birth in 1895. It is an amazingly rich evocation of London in the Eighteen Nineties that invites comparison with Dickens. Indeed, the first three volumes of the sequence[2] include details of proletarian life otherwise only to be found in Tressell's *The Ragged-Trousered Philanthropists* or in Gissing. This is a tram driver: 'a bitter dew had lain upon his lashes, stinging the lids of his eyes, vulnerable to detritus falling from one or other of a hundred thousand chimneys of South London'. *The Dark Lantern* is crucial in its statement of the groundbass of the sequence: with the passing of power from the land to the City of London, money has got into the wrong hands. The distress caused by industrialisation has been exacer-

bated by Free Trade. English farming has been hard hit.
'From the land which is the mother of the race go the
children to the towns, with their cheap food, foreign produce of peasants paid but a few pence a week to produce
that food, which is bought by the financiers of the City of
London, who virtually control the economies of those
foreign countries, for their own profit. These financiers
also control the exports of our factories, in which the
rosy-faced countryman has gone, in a few years to lose his
health and his stability of living, which before was
balanced in natural work upon the soil.'

That is from the journal of Phillip's grandfather,
Richard's father, that Richard peruses while his wife is in
labour with Phillip. Richard's father had to sell the
family land in Dorset because of financial problems
aggravated by Free Trade. This means that Richard
works as a clerk in the City. It means that Phillip is born
and brought up in Wakenham (Lewisham).

The extracts from the journal of Phillip's grandfather
are seminal. They contain the germ of Phillip's political
ideas. (It would be fascinating to discover whether such a
journal existed or whether it was concocted by Williamson, with borrowings from Richard Jefferies.)

'The sinister migration from the land to the towns, this
spoliation of the true wealth of the nation, which is the
health and strength of its people and the fertility of its
mother soil, where will it end? Who will stay its down-
ward rush upon the slopes of Gadarene? When will a
prophet arise to lead the people back to their natural
heritage, before the nation shall perish even as ancient
Rome? Such a prophet will have to face, like David, not
only the towering strength of Goliath, which is *laissez-
faire* and the so-called inevitability of progress implanted
in the minds of the millions who cannot help themselves,
but the entire power of the money massed in the vaults of
the City of London. What fate befell even the Son of

God, when He turned over the tables of the money changers in the Temple, we know from the sad reading of Holy Scripture.' Thus Phillip's admiration for Hitler and his support of Sir Hereward Birkin (Sir Oswald Mosley) were determined by his family history. *A Chronicle of Ancient Sunlight* is a novel of cause and effect.

The aim behind the *Chronicle* is to analyse one European family to show how lovelessness, the estrangement produced by industrial civilisation, leads to war. The young Phillip, denied love by his father, finds himself in nature. 'At home and at school he was someone else, doing and saying things that had nothing to do with what he really was.' The withering effect on Phillip of the lovelessness produced in Richard by *his* father is paralleled by the encroaching of the London County Council on Wakenham. An oak tree in a park is blighted. The vicar explains to Phillip: 'There was something about smoke drifting from the factories in the old marshland south of the river, and the acid dust in the atmosphere, which hung low with fog from the Thames and slowly poisoned the leaves of the oak. So it was stunted, fighting all the time for pure air, just like a human being.' (*Young Phillip Maddison*)

When Phillip leaves school he works as an insurance clerk in the City. He joins the Territorials. In August 1914 he volunteers. His father's sister Dora, Hellenist and suffragette, realises the war is a 'European Industrialists' war, for markets, Germany being the latest competitor.' She sees the wrongness of a war between the cousin nations Germany and Britain. Her mother, Phillip's grandmother, was German.

Phillip's first experience of action kills his illusions about the romance of war. This is his first night in the trenches: '. . . Phillip was aware of moaning in front, and repeated cries like *mutter-mutter-mutter!*, until with amazement . . . he realised that the cries of the German

wounded were the same as *mother, mother, mother!*
heard from the Iron Colonel's bloodless lips just before he
had opened his eyes wide, and died. It was a startling
thought, that the Germans felt like that, too — he hardly
dare think it.' (*How Dear Is Life*)

Six weeks later Phillip takes part in the Christmas
Truce. It is the central event of his life. He discovers that
the German soldiers think they are fighting for exactly
the same things as the British. So the war was a misunderstanding or a failure to understand. It was possible for
both sides to be right in a dispute.

Phillip is commissioned, wounded. He experiences
comradeship. His county regiment is 'one large happy
family'. It provides a substitute for his unhappy childhood. The comradeship is generated out of proximity to
death. It includes respect for the enemy. It is an attitude
which the civilian, exhorted by propaganda, is incapable
of understanding. When Phillip goes on leave, he is even
more isolated from his family than before.

Comparable in effect to the Christmas Truce is
Phillip's discovery via his cousin Willie Maddison soon
after the war of *The Story of My Heart* by Richard
Jefferies. It is a revelation. As Willie Maddison, Phillip's
alter ego and fictional prototype, explains in *The
Pathway*, the last volume of the *Flax of Dream*, the
tetralogy published between 1921 and 1928: 'I thought
that Jefferies was with me, and of me. I grew and grew
in spiritual strength; and I realised that all the world
was built up of thought; that the ideals which animated
the world, were but thought; mostly mediocre and
selfish thought. Change thought, and you change the
world.'

Williamson's debt to Jefferies is considerable. Jefferies
is responsible for the sunlight motif that permeates both
the tetralogy and the *Chronicle*. Ancient sunlight 'arises
again as Truth'. It stands for a kind of metempsychosis.

As Jefferies wrote: 'I am in the midst of eternity; it is all about me in the sunshine.'

At the end of the war part of Phillip's essence remains frozen in Flanders with his dead friends. 'His heart had opened to all life through the friends he had known in the war.' He is aware of his obligations as a survivor. He must 'write the greatest novel about the war'. In the Nineteen Twenties Phillip writes the Donkin tetralogy. He muses in his journal:

A child should be allowed to grow itself naturally. The parent's influence should be indirect; the child should learn by the divine instinct of imitation, not by the human vice of compulsion. Everywhere in the world is compulsion, instead of inspired discipline; so everywhere in the world is lack of harmony. There can be no harmony, or attempt to create it widely, until the internecine financial system is made the servant, and not allowed to remain the master, of human destiny. Julian, and Porky and yes, myself— are in various ways trying to writhe out of the coils of childhood's upbringing. If I can reveal the past of one human being—Donkin—truly, clearly, objectively, then the causes of personal unrest, which are the causes of strife in the world between individuals, masses, nations, will be made plain for the first time in human history. Only a novel of character, of many characters each of whose thoughts and actions is based on pure cause and effect, will be of any use to the world in the future.

(*The Innocent Moon*)

Phillip's cousin Willie tells of the German cemeteries in Flanders: acres of black crosses bereft of flowers: 'What ferocious mind had ordered such a revenge . . . Here was hate; here was the crystallized mentality of a declining European civilization; here was the frustration of love that was the Great War!' The connection is made between this hate and 'a decadent financial system that allows nearly three million men to rot on the dole in Great Britain alone'.

And Germany? From Willie Maddison's notebooks, Munich 1923:

The inflation has ruined all classes in Germany. Jews arrive daily from the ghettoes of Poland with a few roubles and become property owners of houses, streets of houses, small businesses, and firms, almost overnight. The *morale* of a nation, depressed by defeat, is temporarily destroyed. A phrase used by Sir Eric Geddes, who at the outbreak of war was a railway manager in England and ended a Cabinet Minister, is often repeated in my hearing. 'Germany is a lemon to be squeezed until the pips squeak.'

The pips are more than squeaking. They are shrieking. They shriek through one man's voice. He has the truest eyes I have ever seen in a man's face, he is an ex-corporal of the Linz Regiment, which opposed my regiment under Messines hill on Christmas Day, 1914. We made a truce then, which must never be broken.

(Lucifer Before Sunrise)

Phillip is depressed by the failure of the General Strike in 1926, 'a mass demand for a decent life'. 'A European generation had died upon the battlefields in vain.' The feeling is akin to that of Sassoon's *A Case for the Miners*. He is elated by the Labour victory in 1929. Realising that 'it's the international money system which rules the world', Phillip wonders if human nature would be 'perfectible under a balanced economic system'. One of the junior ministers in the Labour Government is Sir Hereward Birkin. When the Cabinet rejects his proposals to end unemployment, he resigns. Phillip reads his speech of resignation in a newspaper:

Why is it right and desirable that British capital should go overseas to equip factories to compete against us, and by means of sweated labour to undercut our prices, to build roads in the Argentine or Timbuktoo, while it is supposed to shake the whole basis of our financial strength if anyone dares to suggest

the raising of money by the government of this country to pro-
vide work for the people of this country?

(*The Phoenix Generation*)

Birkin eventually forms the Imperial Socialist Party.
Phillip approves of Birkin's ideas for the regeneration of
England. He is present at a dinner party at which Birkin
says:

Our aim is nothing less than a great efflorescence of Western
civilization, based on true values of the human spirit . . . Our
party works for the transcendence of the little ego which cowers
within all of us at times, a feeble spirit blown hither and thither
by every gust of transient political manoeuvring . . . when we of
the Imperial Socialist Party come to power, the first thing we
shall do is to forbid the export of British capital abroad. Then
we shall command the means, which is the finance, to develop
our great inheritance.

(*The Phoenix Generation*)

Meanwhile in Germany there is Hitler, ' "a phoenix from
the chaos of the battlefields, a messiah" '. Phillip is
invited to a Nuremberg rally. In Berlin he talks to a
young Nazi: 'I had a cousin who had a great admiration
for Hitler. He was here just after the war. He saw Hitler
as someone who could save Germany, and the world.
Hitler, he told me, had perceived the root-causes of war
in the unfulfilled human ego, and was striving to alter
this by creating a new, truly human world.' In Berlin
Phillip is impressed: 'Everywhere he saw faces which
looked to be breathing extra oxygen: people free from
mental fear. What a difference from the strained faces in
certain parts of London!' Hitler's wish is peace for a thousand years and the creation in the West of the greatest
civilization the world has ever seen. Hitler, for Phillip,
becomes Faustus 'trying to bring a millennium of youth to
the dying Western world'. The rally is a magnificent pre-

Visconti set-piece, complete with Frank Buchman and the Mitford sisters. Seeing Hitler at close quarters in the Party headquarters hotel, Phillip wonders is he 'A Shelley self-driven by an inner tyranny to strike evil? Or a saint who will never draw the sword?' Because of the economic boycott of Germany and the lack of German gold reserves, Hitler begins a barter system to obtain the wheat that Germany lacks because of its sandy soil. Like the economic policies of Napoleon, this poses a threat to the City of London. Birkin prophesies to Phillip: 'The obsolescent financial system will go to war to preserve itself.'

In the early Nineteen Twenties Phillip had married Barley:

He was part of her, she of him; they were one in spirit. How vain and unreal was his former conception of love, arising from longing. With her beside him he shed the shuck of experience, to exist within a freedom which, before he had truly known her, had lain always beyond the horizon of life.

With her he felt himself to be of the very air of the shore, of the light of the ocean, without body, beyond desire.

(*It Was The Nightingale*)

Barley dies in childbirth and Phillip marries Lucy. He does not share with her 'true likeness of thought', Jefferies's definition of love. An attempt to run the family farm for an uncle is a failure, and Phillip, Lucy, and their children move to Devon. Then, in the late Nineteen Thirties, Phillip decides to farm in Norfolk. His regeneration of a derelict farm will be his contribution towards the realisation of Birkin's dream. Despite the success of *The Water Wanderer*, a book about an otter that has brought him fame, Phillip is dissatisfied with his career as a writer. 'I'm getting on for forty-one', he says to Lucy, 'and nothing done of my *real* life work.' Phillip faces a daily struggle between the urge to write and the need to supervise a farm bedevilled by hands who will not do what they are told.

Phillip is obsessed by the need to avert another war. His reasons echo those of his Aunt Dora in 1914: 'One more European war will . . . wreck Western culture based on the Greek ideal. Greece was wrecked by rivalries between city states, and the barbarians moved in.' Again: 'I do not want to see another generation of British youths in their graves . . . I do not want to see German or Polish dead or French dead, while Oriental Commissars wait, like jackals, to grow fat on the killings.' Near the end of August 1939, Phillip believes that if he flies to see Hitler he can, as one ex-serviceman to another in the spirit of Christmas Day 1914, persuade him not to go to war. Phillip has regarded Hitler as 'the only true pacifist in Europe'. Has not Hitler said: 'Whoever lights the torch of war in Europe can hope for nothing but chaos . . .' But Hitler has also said: 'Germany must export or die; and Germany shall not die.' Driving up to London, Phillip reflects that the public do not know the real reason for the guarantee to Poland, the extensive British investments in that country. As Phillip enters London, Williamson draws together the defects of a civilisation that is about to go to war yet again. The tone is reminiscent of Céline:

They reached the area left ugly by the maulings of London: speculative hire-purchase housing 'estates'—all trees cut down—tens of thousands of cubic yards of coke-breeze blocks and pink heaps of fletton bricks piled up. Life is big business, fornication, and death. Civilization is chromium fittings, radio, love with pessary, rubber girdles, B.B.C. gentility and the sterilizing of truth, cubic international-type of concrete architecture. Civilization is white sepulchral bread, gin and homosexual jokes in the Shaftesbury Avenue theatres. Civilization is world-citizenship and freedom from tradition, based on rootless eternal wandering in the mind that had nothing to

lose and everything to gain including the whole world. Hoard-
ings, brittle houses, flashiness posing as beauty, mongrel living
and cosmopolitan modernism, no planning, all higgledy-
piggledy—thus the spiritual-material approaches to London,
the great wen Cobbett called it. Was the wen about to burst
and pus run throughout the body politic for the second time in
his life?

(*The Phoenix Generation*)

But Phillip is too late. The next day the Nazis seize the
Danzig customs.

Phillip farms throughout the war. After Dunkirk he is
briefly arrested under Regulation 18B. Back at home,
with France defeated and England under threat of in-
vasion, Phillip and his family worry whether a light will
disturb a nest of swallows. Genius or folly? It is reminiscent of what E. M. Forster wrote of T. S. Eliot and the
appearance of *Prufrock* in 1917, 'preserving a tiny drop
of our self-respect', carrying on 'the human heritage'.
Phillip, like Birkin, thinks that England should make
peace with Germany, to leave Hitler free to defeat Russia.
(Although Phillip loathes war, he has no regrets about
dead Russians, or even, until nearly the end of the war,
about dead Jews.) Hitler is not anti-British. Why else
were the German tanks halted before Dunkirk? Phillip
compares Hitler at this stage of the war to Jefferies.
Hitler, too, has 'the conception of an ideal world beyond
human limits: the world that would roll back upon and
crush him: Sisyphus.' (*A Solitary War*)

For Phillip it is 'a Cads' War', 'a mass exhibitionism of
Europeans with damaged personalities; Churchill versus
Hitler.' 'They were all mad in the war except the young
who were facing death for civilian stupidity; but few knew
it. The British moaned about Coventry, while the R.A.F.
bombed innumerable civilians, old and young, in phosphorus raids upon one artisan suburb after another in all
the major German towns, night after night, week after

week, month after month . . .' (*Lucifer Before Sunrise*)

Wagnerian imagery articulates Hitler's fall. As war began in 1914 Phillip heard 'most beautiful music' at home. 'It made him think of the sun, which was dying, and saying goodbye to the earth, a golden god slain in the darkness.' It was the *Liebestod* from *Tristan und Isolde*. In late 1939 Phillip listens on the wireless to a Wagner concert from Berlin: 'The music of the Flower Garden in *Parsifal* took him away to a world of dream in which beauty, nobility, loyalty and truth were one. He lay back in his chair, feeling that one day this truth would be paramount in the world.' Ploughing, he thinks: 'This was the twilight of the gods, who were falling, mankind with them.' Hitler is Siegfried: 'the pure hero had, through arrogance, betrayed himself and all about him.' Lucifer the morning star, the light-bringer, had become the fallen angel, the prince of darkness.

Visiting London in June 1944, Phillip is agreeably surprised: 'the congestion and shadiness of an unplanned City was relieved a little by the catharsis of high explosive.' He is delighted to find birds and wild flowers in the ruins around St. Paul's. The blitz has been revenge on money. The City has been purified by fire. Phillip reasons that ironically the war will mean New York superseding London as world financial centre. It will boost British farming, because there are no longer enough gold reserves with which to import food.

Phillip in his journal as Germany surrenders: 'The barrier against the East is down. Of the European cousin-nations locked in a death-struggle for so long, one is dead, the other bled pallid. The hopes that have animated, or agitated my living during the past thirty years and four months are dead.' He comes to see that the death of Hitler, his *Doppelgänger*, means his reprieve. 'The scapegoat of so much negative living, so much active frustration, is dead.' His hopes since Christmas Day 1914 are dead; the farm having failed, he must now begin his novel sequence. 'Writing is the only thing left to live for.' Alone in Devon, he finds that the elements have renewed in him the wonder of life that he possessed before 1914. As he now sees the past with clarity, he must begin to write about it.

The Gale of the World, the culmination of the sequence, is suffused with the bleakness of the immediate post-war, 'a subconscious fear that never again would life be lived in contentment'. There is, for Phillip, the 'farce' of the trials of German war criminals. 'It seemed that, among the Allies, there were no war criminals. That would be left to history to decide.' Phillip is living alone in a hut on Exmoor, and trying to begin his novel. The nub of this final volume is the thesis of Sir Hereward Birkin's—that is, Sir Oswald Mosley's—book *The Alternative*, that, with the failure of Fascism and Financial Democracy, the solution is 'Europe a Nation'.

Melissa Wilby, the daughter of Lord and Lady Abeline, whom Phillip has known since she was a child, has known since her childhood that Phillip and she were destined for one another. 'Her mind moved to Phillip's vision, as revealed in his books, its confluence with Birkin's thought . . . the firm belief in the positive, creative evolution of man: service not *in vacuo*, as priests in their devotions, but an amalgam of creative science with the Christendom of tomorrow, which would fulfil and fortify Man's deepest aspirations. Eugenics must raise the general level of intelligence to a higher empathy, or Man would meet his doom through malevolent application of the strayed "wonders" of science.'

These ideas are echoed in the rich vein of parapsychology that runs through the book.

The 'gale of the world' is provided by the River Lyn, swollen by a freak storm, flooding Lynmouth. Lightning knocks Phillip unconscious by a funeral pyre he has

prepared for his father's ashes. He experiences a phan-
tasmagoria of scenes of his life, emerging from which is
like 'coming out of Hades'. He awakes and sees a stag and
two hounds huddled together for warmth. The catharsis
of nature provides a synthesis. Then lightning ignites the
funeral pyre.

The curse of lovelessness is thus lifted. Melissa and
Phillip are brought together: Ariel and Prospero. ' "You
have brought love to me",' Phillip tells her; — ' "love
which dissolves arrogance and hatred — love by which one
can see all things as the sun sees them; without shadows".'
Melissa quotes the peroration to *The Alternative*, about
'the final order of the European'. Phillip can now begin
his real life's work. 'I hope in a very small way to complement Birkin's dream by writing my novels.' He realises
that the novels would have been angry and satirical if he
had written them in the Thirties. 'Now I think I can
understand every kind of man and woman. Particularly
my father.' The coda fuses Phillip's vision of his father
and his dark lantern, in the opening chapter of the
Chronicle, and his 'friends in ancient sunlight'.

How has art been made out of such seemingly intract-
able, not to say unfashionable, material? For Williamson
is clearly one more notable twentieth century writer, like
Pound, Yeats, Eliot, D. H. Lawrence, Rebatet,[3] and
Céline, who has gone against the current of history. His
debt to Spengler will have been noticed. He shares
Céline's pacifism, although for different reasons, and his
loathing for contemporary civilisation, but not his anti-
semitism. Céline welcomed Hitler because he promised
destruction, catharsis. But for Williamson/Maddison,
Hitler betrayed himself by going to war; the light-bringer
became a bloody tyrant. In *What is Literature?* Sartre
said that 'No one could suppose for an instant that it
would be possible to write a good novel in praise of anti-
semitism.' Yet one volume in Williamson's sequence, *The*

Phoenix Generation (although it is wrong to prise one book out of the whole, as the sequence is one novel published for convenience in sections), is a 'good novel' in praise of Mosley and Hitler in the Nineteen Thirties. (Williamson's preface to the one-volume edition of the *Flax of Dream* series, published in 1936: 'I salute the great man across the Rhine, whose life symbol is the happy child.') Phillip's reactions in his visit to Germany in 1935 are often naive. Eating in a Berlin restaurant, he learns that it is owned by Jews: 'This surprised Phillip, who, while knowing what he considered to be the distortional magnification of the newspapers, nevertheless had been affected by the reiterations of hostile criticisms of the Nazis. He had thought vaguely of all Jews hiding in cellars, or being held in concentration camps.'

Such a passage, and there are others, obviously begs a plethora of questions.

What is the proper response of a reader to a character who praises Birkin/Mosley and his ideas so fulsomely? Was George Orwell right when he wrote, in *The Lion and the Unicorn*, that 'One would have to look a long time to find a man more barren of ideas than Sir Oswald Mosley. He was as hollow as a jug. Even the elementary fact that Fascism must not offend against national sentiment had escaped him'? How could Mosley's ideas for the regeneration of England based on exploitation of the Empire be squared with the fact that British free speech and comparative high standard of living rested on what Louis MacNeice called 'gagged and impoverished subject peoples'?

There are also questions of fact. In *The Phoenix Generation* it is stated that in August 1939 'British corn prices suddenly dropped over 100 per cent in price, because much of the corn harvest of Central Europe had been bought by a group of financiers in the City of London to prevent it going to Germany by barter.' Where is the evidence of this purchase? There is also the matter of Phillip's support of Quisling. 'One day his name will be cleared.' And of Marshal Pétain and King Leopold of the Belgians. Williamson says that history will vindicate them. Has it? Will it? But perhaps such questionings miss a point. *A Chronicle of Ancient Sunlight* is not life, but a novel, a fiction, an autonomous work of the imagination. Williamson builds a mythopoeic structure out of twentieth century history, but the novel is *not* twentieth century history.

Again, what is the proper response when Phillip, asked in the late autumn of 1939 if his own country isn't good enough for him, replies: 'It will be when all farms are flourishing again, when the soil's fertility is being conserved instead of raped, when village life is a social unity, when pride of craftsmanship returns, when everyone works for the sake of adding to the beauty and importance of life, when every river is clean and bright, and the proud words "I serve" are in everyone's heart and purpose. Then my own country will be good enough for me.' As Orwell said, in *Inside the Whale*, of Lawrence's idealisation of the Etruscans: 'It is a species of defeatism, because that is not the direction in which the world is moving.'

A Chronicle of Ancient Sunlight is, as Phillip said his novel would be, a novel of cause and effect. As the extracts from his grandfather's journal show, everything in Phillip's development was determined by his family history. Viewed objectively, a survivor from Flanders expecting the creation of a land fit for heroes, and finding only lack of concern inside Parliament, might be excused for supporting an extra-Parliamentary movement that promised action, especially when that movement was led by Sir Oswald Mosley, the most gifted politician to emerge in Britain in the Nineteen Twenties. Recent historians have praised Stanley Baldwin for being mediocre, for being such a perfect reflection of the temper of England in the Nineteen Thirties. Such cynicism should not obscure the fact that the only politicians of calibre in England in the Nineteen Thirties, Mosley, Churchill, and Lloyd George, were all out of office. This dearth of talent was due to the Great War. Fascism, as Williamson admitted, was 'a phenomenon of the Western Front'. Yet Phillip Maddison is no fascist. It is not a paradox to say that the only fascist thing about him and his creator was their support of Birkin/Mosley and the Imperial Socialist Party/British Union of Fascists.

Mosley is supposed to have made a private comment on Williamson: 'He will take it all so seriously.'[4] If this is authentic, it reveals Mosley as a true politician, but it also suggests that Williamson's view of politics was too high-minded. There was no need of Lord Butler's reminder that politics is the art of the possible. Politics is not the place, Phillip comes to admit in *Lucifer Before Sunrise*, for 'men of genius, with spiritual power to bring clarity to human beings who are not cynical'. Such men (Hitler, Mosley) should be 'artists in detachment, to shine upon the world as the sun which sees no shadows: whether of the Jew upon the Place of Skulls or upon the smoking corpse lying in the shattered garden of the Berlin Chancellery'.

Phillip Maddison's avowed wish being to write 'a novel of our times, transcending *War and Peace*,' it is instructive to compare *A Chronicle of Ancient Sunlight* with the criticisms Phillip makes of Tolstoy's book. Tolstoy, Phillip says, did not understand Napoleon or why he had gone to war. 'The original impulse of genius, the vision of Napoleon clenched to his clear and unequivocal will-power, where did it appear, in character, upon the pages of the book?' If the *Chronicle* is judged on its understanding of the genius of Hitler, then it is a success, treating

him as it does in a different way from a biographer like
Alan Bullock. Phillip also feels that 'Tolstoy's powers of
endurance were fatigued by the time he arrived at the
third volume, where he argued and propagated ideas
rather than recreated life as it was'. This reverts to the
criticism of Williamson's sometimes excessive use of his
journals. Where Williamson *is* found wanting, in a comparison with Tolstoy, is in the creation of female
characters. The *Chronicle* is void of a Natasha or an
Anna. Many of the women in the *Chronicle* are little
more than symbols, a few traits bundled together and
trotted out each time the character comes on stage, in the
manner of Dickens. Yet this is not such a disadvantage as
it might seem, given that the *Chronicle* is pre-eminently
the story of Phillip Maddison. The women are two-
dimensional because that is how Phillip sees them. It is an
integral part of his *Weltanschauung*. The flaw of egotism
matters less in him than in his creator.

In his journal Phillip writes of his proposed novel: 'My
subject is no less than the dilemma of Western man,
viewed from all aspects with sympathy and precision.'
And: 'I shall reveal the European nerve-rot in the story of
one family: in their mental attitudes towards the truth.'
Phillip's experiences are seen to be the essential experiences of twentieth century man. He embodies the
Zeitgeist. The struggle to farm in Norfolk is a microcosm
of the European macrocosm; the failure of Phillip to
change the ideas of his farm-hands is the failure of Hitler.
It is thus that Phillip experiences all the suffering of the
Second World War in himself. A novel profuse in details
of farming in Norfolk might seem unprepossessing
material for a novel claiming to be universal. It might
seem parochial. The *Chronicle* is about as parochial as
The Iliad. By farming, Phillip was denying his intuition,
his real self, as Hitler did by becoming a man of action.
Out of multiple failure Williamson creates a parable of

creation. 'My story,' Phillip notes, 'shall be the triumph of creative will.'

Not the least of the novel's merits is as a social panorama, fifty years of English life, reminiscent of the treatment of nineteenth century Spain in the *Episodios Nacionales* of Galdós. Williamson's huge structure is held together by subterranean cross-referencing manifest as piercing resonances. At the end of *The Dark Lantern* the old man Pooley, who was born in 1793 and remembers Waterloo, saves the baby Phillip's life by providing ass's milk. Hitler invades Russia and Phillip reads *War and Peace*, and Pooley is recalled, not on the page but in the reader's mind, revealing Phillip against the flux of history. Again, when Dresden is bombed, all the animals in the zoo escape. This recalls the election-night party at Selfridge's in 1929 when a kangaroo boxing in a ring escapes into the crowd; a symbol of the lurking violence that would find its apotheosis at Dresden and Hiroshima. The death of Phillip's mother coincides with the Wagnerian fate of the Crystal Palace.

Among the many profound comments on the maladies of an industrial civilization is 'Mister' à Court Smith, who has 'never done any work'. Each night he puts on headphones (it is in the Nineteen Twenties) to listen to the nightingale before Big Ben and the Stock Exchange Prices. He hopes to hear that some mines, 'shares in which he had bought in 1903, and from which no dividend had been paid since 1904, were to be reopened'. The decadence of the *rentier* class is symbolised by Lucy's (Maddison's second wife's) family, the Coplestons, 'the lazy ruling class which had always put money first . . . their indifference and apathy had ruined England.' The Coplestons possess a painting by Blake. They regard it as ugly, and refuse to believe it is of value. It is kept hidden, and becomes the home of a spider. The *rentier* class is also implicitly damned when 'Teddy' Pinnegar finds Jef-

A Confrontation. Henry at an Anti-Vietnam War Demonstration: London, Downing Street, 1960's

feries's poignant *Hodge and his Masters* 'damn rotten boring tripe'.

Williamson's style eschews Jamesian orotundities. Especially when describing nature or war, it is capable of great flights. In *Love and the Loveless*, for example, there is an astonishing transcendental passage when Phillip revisits the terrain where he and his platoon attacked on the first day of the Somme. In *A Solitary War* and *Lucifer Before Sunrise* there is the haunting contrast of nature and war. The brief final sentence of *Lucifer Before Sunrise* sums up the entire experience of the Second World War: 'Night had come to the western hemisphere.' The style throughout is English in its workmanlike bluffness that is deceptive because of the layers of feeling underneath. In this, Williamson might be likened to Elgar, and a comparison made of *A Chronicle of Ancient Sunlight* and Elgar's symphonies: English attempts to contain a totality of experience.

Williamson regarded himself as a prophet, a man with a message. As a prophet, he is comparable to Blake; as an artist to Tolstoy, Dostoievsky, or Melville. Given the English prejudice against literary gigantism, it is not surprising that Williamson's epic has aroused more interest in the U.S.A. The *Chronicle*, however, has more in common with *Buddenbrooks*, or Musil's *The Man Without Qualities*, than with any English or American work. It *is* a novel 'to rival Tolstoy'. People still upset by the political views of Maddison/Williamson might ponder what George Orwell wrote in a letter to John Middleton Murry in 1944: 'I can respect anyone who is willing to face unpopularity, however much I disagree with him.'

NOTES

1. In Kenneth Allsop's B.B.C. television film-interview with Henry Williamson, Williamson, talking of his novel

Henry Williamson with Oswald Jones. Aylesford Priory, 1960's

Lucifer Before Sunrise, says: '. . . Phillip, who is myself, has a tremendous gap between his ideals and what is.' Cf. text of this interview printed in *The Listener*, 8.ii.1968.

2. *The Dark Lantern, Donkey Boy, Young Phillip Maddison.*
3. Lucien Rebatet, author of *Les Deux Etendards*, which George Steiner regards as 'the greatest novel written in French after Proust'. Cf. letter from Dr. Steiner in *The Times Literary Supplement*, 22.iv.1977.
4. Cf. Daniel Farson, 'Recognising Henry Williamson', in the *Daily Telegraph Magazine*, 28.ii.1975.

ANCIENT SUNLIGHT

Oswald Jones

THERE ARE three works of Henry Williamson that I consider to be the flowers of his total work and to reflect the essence of his being: *Salar the Salmon, Tarka the Otter*, and *The Patriot's Progress*. Although written and published after these three books, his great fifteen-volume *Chronicle*, in which he charted the total experience of his life until the date of the final volume (he usually revised in the light of experience) serves as the ground base from which the others flowered. *Salar*, which flows as do the rivers Taw and Torridge in which the salmon spawned and lived. *Tarka*, with its excitement and climax paralleling those of the chase described. And *The Patriot's Progress*, Henry's earlier war book, with its spare staccato style sounding like the battlefields of his youth; a style which, to the disappointment of many, he did not continue to develop.

These are the blossoms that come from the total experience described in the later books; *Salar* from the quiet contemplation of the rivers and the salmon, and *Tarka* from the contemplation of the countryside, the keeping of a pet otter, and from active participation in following the hounds. And perhaps, for the author, the most exotic of all, a desert flower growing from the wilderness of his war experience, *The Patriot's Progress*.

These books are a distillation of the *observed* experience so fully documented in *A Chronicle of Ancient Sunlight*, which also includes the rest of Henry's life experience, the stem, the leaves, the roots, and the very soil of it nurtured by the life and works of Richard Jefferies, which were so fundamental to Henry's concept of 'Ancient Sunlight'. As a young man he had been profoundly affected by Jefferies's spiritual, mystical autobiography, *The Story of My Heart*. Jefferies's other works, the essays and novels of the countryside, had a decisive effect on his choice of subject material for his own work. Jefferies was writing of the time immediately prior to Henry's birth, a period on which, as can be seen from *The Dark Lantern*, the first book in the *Chronicle*, he looked back with an affectionate nostalgia.

Henry never, to my knowledge, defined his concept of 'Ancient Sunlight'. My own definition, at least with respect to the *Chronicle*, is the recalling of memories once forgotten, a nostalgic anamnesis. But it is more than that, perhaps a racial anamnesis somewhat akin to C. G. Jung's concept of the Collective Unconscious, but experienced in a more consciously ecstatic light. It is a fixing of experience in time, like a fly in amber existing for all time for others to share, albeit just a glimmer of the original experience.

In spite of his extraordinary power of observation and his faculty for recording clearly what he saw, Henry was a subjective writer whose chief, self-imposed, task was the interpretation of personal experience, not autobiographically but, to use his own term, autopsychically. He has written that men should 'see as the sun sees, without shadows'. That is how he tried to see, from *within*, from the source of light itself, the source of all things. By shadows he meant the dark side of things; but to see without shadows is to see two-dimensionally. He was not too much aware of the subconscious springs of his being. His not wanting to see the shadows shows that he was uninterested in or averse to the unconscious, which must exist and cannot be eliminated. Perhaps it was because he was not consciously aware of his motives that he was able to write so subjectively, especially of women.

The women in Henry's works are two-dimensional, without substance, and all have a strong family resemblance, as if they all came from the same mould, or at least from the same craftsman, for each of them is a projection of the feminine aspect of Henry himself, his Anima. It is not that they are ideal versions of actual women in Henry's life; they are versions of his ideal, animated within a framework taken from life.

In life he did not search for a woman who conformed to his Anima. This was, perhaps, on the one hand an acceptance of reality; but on the other hand he tried to project his ideal onto actual women. This had disastrous results for the relationship when he met women of distinct personality. But often he was attracted by young girls with still unformed personalities. At these times he was probably happiest in a relationship, for his Anima had as much licence to form a romantic ideal of the girl as it had with his fictional women. Or at least for a year or two; either until the girl developed a distinct personality of her own or else severed the friendship in order to do so.

In his relationships Henry was both gentle and authoritarian, an inextricable mixture. His authoritarianism derived from his belief that it is possible to learn from the experience of others and thereby create a more 'perfect' society in its microcosmic and by extension its macrocosmic forms. This belief would lead naturally to the idea of an élitist society, excluding as it must those that learn most from personal experience. His political beliefs were here linked intimately to his own being, and this placed a certain strain on the people close to him, and especially on those who loved him. His authoritative attitudes took an active form, in that he was inclined to try to modify the behaviour of others in a variety of circumstances.

For Henry there was a right way to do all things, and many wrong ways. A trivial instance in my own experience will serve to illustrate this. I was once driving him from Aylesford Priory to the station, to catch a certain train. Somewhere on the way I came to a halt, pulling on the handbrake and allowing the retaining ratchet to give an audible click all the way up, until it was secure. Henry very politely gave me a short lecture on how such a way of applying the handbrake would wear out the cogs, and how the best way was to press the release button when applying it, in the same way that one does when releasing it. My own unspoken view was that my Mini would be worn out long before the ratchet cogs of its handbrake; but to have debated the point with Henry would have been for him tantamount to criticism. Nor did I want to be responsible for missing his train and having to cope with an irritable Henry until the next one.

There really was for Henry only one correct way to do anything, even something so simple as washing dishes. One day after lunch, when he was staying with me at Rowlstone Mill in Herefordshire, he tried to organise a somewhat haphazard group of fellow guests into an efficient washing-up team, that would not make pools of water on the floor . . .

Politically, it was natural for him to look for a *Leader*, one who would make whole the disorder of the economic structure of society in the late nineteen twenties and thirties. These were very simple but strongly held beliefs, the more so because they were so single-minded, untinged by other ideas. Daniel Farson has written that Henry's consistent support for Sir Oswald Mosley almost certainly 'lost him the honour, a knighthood or the Order of Merit, that must have otherwise been his'. This is surely true. Such honours he would have received gratefully, and the bestowers would have honoured themselves in honouring him. He would not have sought such awards, but representations are known to have been made on his behalf, without success and without his knowledge.

No one should want at this time of day to reopen old

wounds, and there is something ungenerous in continuing to harry people for what they thought, or said, or did, forty or more years ago. Positions sincerely held then are often quite irrelevant to the changed conditions of today. Yet one cannot but, in one's own mind, note the wry contrast between the acclaim bestowed on pre-war 'left-wing' sympathisers and adherents, with their corrosive philosophies — E. M. Forster, W. H. Auden, Harold Laski, John Strachey, and the Webbs, among a host of others — and the treatment received by such an ultra-patriot as Henry Williamson. Anthony Blunt, in spite of his treacherous behaviour, received a knighthood for his services to the arts; Henry Williamson, who equally deserved high honour for his services to literature — to say nothing of his military record in the first war and his services to agriculture in the second — was denied academic or nobiliary recognition in spite of the fact that he put loyalty to his country first when wrestling with his own troubled political conscience.

There was simply not room for Henry Williamson among the commercial and show business honours lists of the Harold Wilson era, which happened to coincide with the period of his life when such recognition was most likely, and in his case due. Charles Chaplin and P. G. Wodehouse had to live into their late eighties and nineties respectively, it would seem, in order to achieve knighthood. But perhaps ultimately Henry Williamson will receive the greater recognition of his works being read when present-day politicians are but names alongside dates in the history books.

I last saw Henry in a nursing home in north-west London, earlier in the year of his death. We walked very slowly arm in arm around the grounds; very slowly, for this was now his pace. I remained cheerful for him then, but could not remain so when I was later asked how he was. He died during the summer and was taken to his home at Ox's Cross, from whence he was taken to George-ham churchyard, to be lowered by his sons into his much loved Devon soil. Now he has become one with his Ancient Sunlight, and with that 'Lost Generation', the dead of 1914-1918, with whom he had kept faith.

SOME NOTES ON 'THE FLAX OF DREAM' AND 'A CHRONICLE OF ANCIENT SUNLIGHT'

Henry Williamson

'THE FLAX' was begun during the last year of the Great War, in 1918. There were two Mss, one of which I destroyed, the other is still in my possession. Both were written out of a secret self which was beginning to withdraw from Army life and living, a secret self of longing and emotion and possibly imbalance. I was ignorant of Literature, having failed to pass the London Matriculation exam in that subject in 1913. My Mss were a mixture of all kinds of moods and hopes and other writers' styles. The theme was of lost love, lost friendship, earthly misunderstandings, resurrection and forgiveness in Elysian Fields. My hero was killed in battle—a commonplace ending of those days—and returned a ghost. At last, those who had misjudged him understood.

A third attempt was made just after the war. The first volume, *The Beautiful Years*, had all the freshness of an early morning of the summers of my boyhood. It was also sad: the father did not understand the son. This book had good reviews. Its successor had very bad reviews. No wonder! It was a slapstick attack on schoolmasters; satiric, 'screamingly funny' to myself, coming down every morning in Skirr Cottage, bare-foot, to sit on the kitchen table and read what had poured forth from me the night before. I yelled with laughter. Ye gods, I was showing them up, my former critics in the classroom! The book

was really a terrible farrago. *John o' London's* said it out-
did Dotheboys Hall. *The Times Literary Supplement* (I
quote from 1922 memory: J. B. Priestley, coming into the
cottage one morning in 1924, advised me to burn my
press-clipping book, so I set fire to it then & there) said,
'He pictures for us meticulously a sordid round of deceit,
subterfuge, and rank bad behaviour', and declared that
the masters were worse than the brats they had to teach.
The book did not reach the sales of the *Beautiful Years*
(520) and was soon remaindered for 6d a copy. It is now a
collector's rare item.

The *Dream of Fair Women* followed. The publishers,
Collins, by this time had also published, on the advice of
J. D. Beresford, two nature books, *The Lone Swallows*,
and *The Peregrine's Saga*. These had been well reviewed,
but had sold about 200 copies each. That brought my
literary career to 1924.

In 1928 Collins wrote they did not wish to exercise their
option on the fourth novel, for £25 advance. Just before
this, I had been told in confidence that *Tarka the Otter*,
(published in October 1927), had won the *Hawthornden
Prize*. I was badly in need of money, and asked them to
accept my novel — almost completed — unseen, and pay
over £25. The novel, I said, was faraway ahead of the
other three: something quite different indeed. An official
in 48 Pall Mall said, gently and kindly, that they did not
want to look at the Mss. 'We are going to return all your
copyrights. I'm sorry, but —'. So I offered the novel to
Constant Huntington of Putnam's, who had done *Tarka*,
for £50. 'But you cannot write novels', he said. I repeated
what I had told Collins & Co. He asked to see the Mss.
This terrified me; I dreaded a negative criticism of a work
held tenuously within the imagination: worse, adverse
criticism, which hurt, delayed, even stopped one. While I
was hoping that he would trust me in my declaration that
the novel would sell, and let me have £50, another

publisher offered my agent £250 for the next book, whatever it was. I did not tell Huntington this, but asked him
again to trust me, adding that I had no money, and had
to support a wife and baby. Indeed I begged him to trust
me, and fork out £50. Nothing doing. I told my agent to
decide. £250 arrived from Jonathan Cape that afternoon.

Alas for the good intentions of the diffident! When
Galsworthy cracked up *Tarka* in the Aeolian Hall in June
1928, Sir Godfrey Collins was heard to say, 'I discovered
this young man'; dear Constant Huntington was aghast,
the announcement came as a surprise to him, as to most
of the 800 people present. In congratulating me, Huntington said, 'Well, genius I suppose has its undependible
side'. *The Pathway*, published four months later, sold
eventually 30,000 copies. It shocked some readers. My
wife's father read it, and on putting the book down,
remarked only that his son-in-law was an ass. There was
some basis for this criticism. *The Church Times*, which
he read, had declared the book to be blasphemous. Maddison, the ex-soldier, was the angry young man of the
post-war, with a political slant to his idealism — 'My aim is
to co-ordinate the teaching of Christ with that of
Lenin' — and a devastating self-distrust, being aware of
the difference between what he preached and what he
did. He could not reconcile the surviving soldier-feelings
with those of the civilian mind at home. He blamed his
nervous, diffident state of mind on his schooling, particularly on the head master. (By this time, *Dandelion Days*,
mixture of *Comic Cuts*, mystical nature, *Beano*, Dotheboys Hall — which I had not read — was fortunately out of
the way). However, I showed them to Cape, saying, 'I am
going to rewrite them'.

Jonathan Cape was advised by his reader, Edward Garnett, not to republish the three earlier novels. Garnett's
report on them was devastating: so when I had recast the
trio I gave them to Faber's — severely cut, altered, and

now in line with the central theme of *Pathway*. They sold
well; *The Flax of Dream* was concluded.

Even at that time I could not be sure that the work, in
its final form, completed when I was under 30, was fun-
damentally true. My feeling was not new: I had it in
1919, hence the escape-route *via* Phillip Maddison, the
London cousin. William Maddison acted as he did
because he had lacked father-love. His mother died
giving birth to him. John and Jenny Maddison had
adored one another. They were entirely suited; they lived
a quiet, happy life, being wholly themselves. Then one
died. The father had known true love; he would all his
life have this love in his being. Surely he would not have
behaved as John Maddison behaved towards Willie, his
little son: whose early life was impressed by a pattern of
incompleteness; lacking the father-hero vision on which
to grow spiritually sound, he made his own wilderness-
vision later, through poetic feeling. It was not the war
which deranged him; but that early pattern, 'poor twisted
boy', ever seeking what was lacking in him, restless,
escapist, hurrying to find over the next hill what he had
not found in life — serenity through love.

However, I had thought of the *Flax* as 'the subjective or
romantic treatment of the theme of redemption, while
the story of Phillip, the poor London cousin, would be
built on the classic or objective pattern'. This wording
was possibly clumsy, but that is how I phrased it to myself
in the early 'twenties. From the summer of 1919, my entire outlook had changed. I knew I was a writer, I knew
my destiny, I was tremulous, like something new born.
The hectic tempo of the infantry war, at home and at the
front, was ended; I became solitary, and dedicate. In this
aspect, the words of William Maddison, when talking to
Mary about his changed state of mind, are more or less
autobiographical. So Phillip came into the four novels of
the *Flax*; he had a watching brief, as it were. To use the

building metaphor, his appearances were intended for ties.

As I have said, *The Pathway*, ultimate volume of the *Flax*, was written between 1924 and 1928, and published in October of that year. Twenty years were to pass before the first sentence of the new series of novels was written. And during those twenty years the proverb of Blake was chronically before my mind, 'He who desires but acts not breeds pestilence'.

The reason for the chronic putting-off lay, I told myself, in the changed circumstance of my living since 1924. Part One of the *Pathway* had been written during the last few weeks of that year, easily, with clear imaginative excitement, and devotion. The book was broken off just before Christmas, which was to be spent in the home of the girl I was going to marry. She was the 'original' of Mary Ogilvie, and her father was Sufford Chychester in the story, Mary's great-uncle. With what joy did I think of the West Country, from the empty house near London in which I had been writing my novel, at night, in the flame of a single candle set in a Cromwellian brass stick! The bare walls and floor boards, the flickering shadows, the coal fire, the garden room where my uncle had died in pain and torment — many years later to arise in Phillip's story as Hugh Turney. At last the third week of December came, and I set off to Devon. In my bag were presents for my new friends, who had accepted me in their midst to take that beautiful, modest, and tender girl for my bride.

One of the presents was a book, which I had bought in town, by the Rev. 'Dick' Sheppard, priest in charge of St. Martin-in-the-Fields, whose services, with his gentle and compassionate voice, were then deeply appreciated by many listeners to 2 L O, the London B.B.C. station at Savoy Hill. But, unknown to me, my father-in-law-to-be had read, in *The Church Times*, a review of the book, which damned it. He was a courteous, kind, gentle old man, but I had never been at ease with him, and anticipating his joy on receiving the book the following morning, I said on that Christmas Eve, 'What do you think of Dick Sheppard, Sir?', for surely he, as a churchwarden of the little barn-like church above the marsh, would be an appreciator.

'Oh, that fellow,' he replied. 'I've no use for him at all,' and the subject was dropped as he took up the latest 3d booklet adventure of Sexton Blake, famous detective, and his assistant Tinker. I hastened away into the town, to buy him a book on Rock Plants, for he was a keen gardener. And alas, so weak was my head, that I allowed an old man's remark to spoil my Christmas; and doubt, too, extended to his daughter. I went for a long walk alone, all the joy of my work in London was gone.

Some readers of *The Pathway* have felt a change of feeling, a strain replacing the spiritual clearness, after Part One, called 'Winter'. I must try and account for this. Originally the ending was not intended to be tragic, with the drowning of William Maddison in the estuary of the Two Rivers. Caught by the tide opposite Appledore, on the Middle Ridge, at night, he was to struggle to keep afloat by willpower, and not to give up. He must return, lest others be hurt further by his death. Eventually the swift flowing currents were to take him inshore, having seen, while he reviewed his life in the waters, how arrogance had darkened his spirit, overlaying its inspiration.

The book was abandoned soon after January, 1925. I was married in May of that year, my qualms, or thoughts of the spirit, set aside. Children came in the following years. Alas there were hopeless attempts to help the deteriorating fortunes of my father-in-law and his sons. I made the mistake of trying to re-pattern their lives for them. By 1928, when the book was resumed, Maddison,

my doppelgänger, had become irritable and haggard, a
ranter at times, immediately remorseful, but doomed by
his own nature. This was a return to the hopeless theme
of the early versions started during the war in 1918, the
same fatalistic pattern. Death was the only clarification.

Twenty years later, another attempt to settle the
family, with the help of one of my wife's brothers, on a
farm in Norfolk failed in the same pattern of failure as
revealed by William Maddison, who saw, at the end of
The Pathway, another way by which the world might
be redeemed — by direct political action. 'We must rouse
the ex-soldiers!' in the manner of the 'ex-corporal in
Germany, with the truest eyes I have seen in any man'.
There it was: the phoenix impulse, 'arisen from the
frozen battlefields of 1914', during the miraculous truce
between German and Briton in No-man's Land. A holy
impulse; which in direct action could only become
changed, for men were different in their minds, and to
make all in one pattern would in itself be tyrannous, and
therefore false. William Maddison knew this, too; and I
think (I do not *know*, the author is but a medium for his
visions and feelings) he went to his death with a presenti-
ment that he had come to the end of his pathway, where
Love would be awaiting him, as for all who try, falter,
and fail, in the after-world.

So much for William Maddison. Why was *The Flax*
written? On what impulse? I felt in 1919 that the gift
within me, or the impulses, came from outside myself,
from the Spiritual World; that I was the trustee for work
which only I could do, to help reveal to others the simple
truth of God underlying all creation.

In my own personal life, from 1926 onwards, until
1945 indeed, and the selling of the farm — a failure to me,
despite what we did in eight years, through many difficulties and dissensions, being said now to be the basis of
the success of those who came after — there was no time to

withdraw oneself, to walk the hills and the shores of sea
and river, to meditate and so bring to being the books
about Phillip. By 1948 the family was settled; amity succeeded dissension. We had been part of the fragmen-
tating war in Europe; now we were recovering. So in
1949, under changed circumstances, *The Dark Lantern*,
the first volume of Phillip's story, was at last started.

The years 1937-1945, although strenuous, —one was
labourer, engineer, business man, manager of a farm of
240 acres with insufficient labour, and insufficient food
for the working men—nevertheless produced some books
and (unpublished) Mss of other volumes. I wrote over a
million words, most of them at night, after the day's work
which started at 5.30 a.m. with feeding of horses, and
ended at 9 p.m. with loading of 15 tons of sugar-beet. It
was a punishing, also cathartic time; the worst part of it
was the feeling of failure, of guilt that one had fallen so
far beneath standards one knew to be right. I was permanently tired, sleepless, often bitter, generally without
hope, seeing myself as but a microcosm of Europe in
travail. Now for the new phase. I had lost self-confidence.
The Dark Lantern was written tremulously. It was hard
to believe that it was not dull (as some critics later
declared!), boring, and dreary. It was a long book; and it
had been commissioned by Messrs Collins, who had, in
the intervening years, felt that it had been a mistake of
their predecessors in office not to take up the original
option. But history repeats itself; perhaps we all do not
change so much as we think we do; and in due course,
dismay was felt that the commissioned novel was not what
it had been hoped to be. The author's fears were confirmed; he was finished. Then, through the intervention
of a friend who was also a publisher's reader and a
believer in the book, it was taken by Macdonald & Co.,
without its being seen by any of the directors. Much
relieved that someone had faith in the work, the author

set to work to leaven or lighten many of the scenes which perhaps had been rather grim; and new chapters were worked in. By this time the book had four beginnings; all appear in the book! *Lantern* originally began with the arrival of Thomas Turney and his profligate son Hugh at Liverpool Street station . . . now the beginning of part 2.

I could not believe that the novel was interesting. Perhaps this is because it was written outside myself, as *Salar the Salmon* was—a hard work, based on study and observation, and made as a sculptor chips away the hard stone.

Now I am working on the seventh volume, which I hope, by discipline and by planning, to end in 1959. A comparatively short book, a soldier's tale. Hitherto the scenes and characters have ruled me; now I must, having established their world, learn the art of leaving out in order to intensify what is left in: an art which Proust, according to Anatole France, never acquired. Often one thinks of the saying of M. France—'Art is long, but Proust is longer'. Proust, as it seems to me, wrote variations on some of his incidents or thoughts and lumped them all in together.

What, I am asked, is the basic feeling, or faith, of my authorship? What impels one to sit, hour after hour, week after week, from autumn to spring, in a hilltop hut in Devon, in the dark days, before a wood fire, and live, sometimes glowingly, in the scenes which arise before one? Is it a neurotic impulse, derived from childhood incapacity to face up to life under a roof which was shadowed, much as Phillip's life was shadowed; and his father Richard's life, in turn, before him? Is this how one seeks prominence, how one justifies oneself in one's own eyes? Shall I confess what I believe deeply within myself? That life is a Spirit; that the artist is but a medium of the Spirit of life; that many, if not all, of his 'imaginative' thoughts and impulses towards magnanimity are as it were signals. The theme of the last published novel, *The Golden Virgin*, is love and the loveless. I wanted the title page to bear that sub-title of *Love and the Loveless*, but was asked to omit it. Of course the percipient reader will live with this underlying theme; that men who have love, which is also Love, the impersonal force of creation, have a sense of honour and comradeship and courage; impersonal love bears them up, their personal love is not selfish; that the lost or bewildered or crooked or unhappy or loveless ones break down, for they have found nothing outside themselves to sustain them, in the hard testing of life, by which the spirit of man is made clear.

I would like to end my apologia with a quotation from a book composed in prison and written shortly after his release by one whose thought has greatly influenced my own: a man who, wounded in 1914 when his aeroplane crashed, is perhaps the most misunderstood man of my generation.

'Our task is to preserve and build. If the Fatherland of Europe is lost, all is lost. That home of the soul of man must be saved by any sacrifice . . . It is the age of decision, in which the long striving of the European soul will reach to fulfilment or plunge to final death.' (Sir Oswald Mosley, *The Alternative*, p.314).

Speaking for myself as a writer, I do not think I could write outside the belief that the purpose of life is to create beauty, 'under the fostering hand of the Creator'. Everybody has his bad or off moments; but there is no happiness, or serenity, without the voidance of self, thus making way for the spirit by which alone an artist can live and have his being.

Autumn 1957

APPENDIX 2
AN AFFIRMATION

Henry Williamson

ATROCITIES are 'news' again, in the World's Press. All wars — particularly 'righteous' wars — are now atrocious. They threaten to make us all moon dust.

More than a quarter of a century ago I stood by a radio set in my Norfolk farmhouse, waiting to hear the end of the 1939-45 war. I had been standing by the illuminated panel for half an hour. All I had heard was a German voice repeating 'Stand by for an important announcement!' Silence followed — then some Wagnerian music.

During that war I had prayed that it should end before 'the two white giants of Europe bleed themselves to death, and Stalinism come to the Channel'.

My notebook was before the yellow panel. I had been locked up, briefly, during 1940, as a suspected traitor. I, who had fought, in 1914, in Flanders with the infantry, and taken part in the truce on Christmas Day, and survived several battles, to return home in 1919.

Of course my name was cleared, as I knew it would be.

My mind was in balance between all combatants during those dark days of 1939-1945. I kept a diary, which would one day be part of history I told myself.

Here follows an extract from what I wrote during that late April morning of 1945, while awaiting news of the war's end from the German rundfunk at Kiel — 'the last resort'.

England must be about the only place where a man might listen to a broadcast from the other side and not be thrown to death by typhus in a concentration camp. Those camps — each one held enough political prisoners from the Eastern camps to fill it a dozen times over. And, supreme in the air, the victors' aircraft have destroyed all sewerage and water systems, all transport by road and rail, so that for weeks hundreds of thousands of men and women have been starving and without medical supplies.

'Stand by for an important announcement!' said a German voice.

Russia is over the Elbe, and is it henceforward to be not so much the Decline of the West as the Renaissance of the East, according to the prophecy of Oswald Spengler in his book written in 1911?

'Stand by for an important announcement!'

The barrier against the East is down. Of the European cousin-nations locked in a death-struggle for so long, one is dead, the other bled pallid. The hopes that have animated or agitated my living since the Christmas truce under Messines hill in Flanders were in vain. Yet the artist must, with his last breath, strive for equipoise.

'Stand by for an important announcement!'

Truth is relative. The horror of innumerable civilians burning in coke ovens called crematoria is the horror of hundreds of thousands of civilians burning in Hamburg, Breslau and other German towns set on fire by the phosphorus bombs of the R.A.F., following a policy inspired by Churchill's 'grey eminence', that while a factory would be rebuilt in eighteen months after destruction, it would take eighteen years to build a worker.

   'La balance, toujours la balance!' My poor Philippe Pétain: it was your mistake not to have remained on the battlefield of Verdun.

'Stand by for an important announcement!'

The horror of Japanese soldiers bayonetting helpless British prisoners of war kneeling with their arms bound is the horror of Japanese soldiers being roasted alive by flame-throwers directed into their foxholes.

Men are killed deliberately by cold-water douches, and deliberately by the breaking of reservoir-dams. The old world of partisanship is no good. Has 'The last Christian died on the Cross'?

'Stand by for an important announcement!'

Still no words follow. Instead, a record of *Siegfried's Funeral March*.

Silence.

Whisperings.

'Here is Grand-Admiral Doenitz to say a few words!'

Doenitz announces that the Führer is fallen.

And at once the thought arose in me: *This lets me out.*

'Germany will fight on!'

What else can he say? He is a dead man speaking for a dying nation. The loud-speaker hissing, the broadcast from Kiel is finished.

The scapegoat of so much negative living, so much active frustration, is dead. The phoenix of the frozen battlefield of Christmas 1914 is, despite all, infirmity. For on that day, so long ago, the men of the volunteer battalion, in which I served, fraternised with the volunteer Linz battalion, in which Hitler served. The friendliness of the Germans was the most radiant memory of my post-war life—perhaps that part of my living that was unnatural.

Now I am, by the grace of God, reprieved.

Wagner saw it all before it happened, with the clarity of genius—from *Rheingold* to Götterdämmerung.

For as the war of universal misery seems almost to have expended itself on the bodies of those who helped to make it, I accept the historical (and poetical) truth that men of genius, with spiritual power to bring clarity to human beings who are not cynical, *must* avoid direct action upon the souls of their fellow-men, and be artists in detachment, to shine upon the world as the sun which sees no shadows, whether of the Jew on the Cross upon the Place of Skulls or upon the smoking corpse lying in the shattered garden of the Berlin Chancery.

Spring 1970

APPENDIX 3

ADDRESS GIVEN AT THE MEMORIAL SERVICE AT ST. MARTIN-IN-THE-FIELDS, LONDON, AT 12 NOON ON THURSDAY, 1 DECEMBER, 1977

Ted Hughes

As a service of mourning, this ceremony belongs properly to Henry Williamson's family. But as a Memorial Service and a Service of Thanksgiving it belongs to all of us.

We have come together today to remember the extra-ordinary vitality, and the long life — productive and energetic almost to the very end — and the genius, of an extraordinary man.

When his daughter Margaret asked me to say some-thing today, I was startled, because there must be quite a few people much better qualified to do this than I am. But I see a kind of logic in it. I hope I shall be forgiven if I speak now of my own feelings, and of my private acquaintance with his work and with him. But Henry Williamson has been such an essential and precious part of my life, in some ways a crucial part, that I can't really speak of him in any other way. And in paying down some of my own debt of gratitude, perhaps I shall speak for many others.

He was three things to me. First one, then two, and finally, late in his life, three.

First of all, as for a very great number of his country-men, he was the inspired author of *Tarka the Otter*. No doubt if he could hear me say that, he would howl with exasperation, because if ever a writer was hounded and hallooed by one of his own creations, Henry was hunted by the fame of that book. As if he had never written anything else. At the same time, he was passionately attached to Tarka. He knew just how important it was for him. In a very real sense, that Devon otter was his totem, something truly sacred to him, deeply and mysteriously kin, and it remained so throughout his life. It may seem odd, but to me he always resembled a fierce otter facially— that fierce, fiercely alert, bristly look. However that may be, it was through his instinctive loyalty to the spirit of that animal that he wrote his most wonderful pages. And it was through that wild creature, too, that he arrived at much in his later beliefs, even much of what many came to regard as his later mistakes.

My own bond with Henry Williamson was made through that book. I was about eleven years old when I found it, and for the next year I read little else. I count it one of the great pieces of good fortune in my life. It entered into me and gave shape and words to my world, as no book ever has done since. I recognised even then, I suppose, that it is something of a holy book, a soul-book, written with the life blood of an unusual poet. Henry knew the same. I remember him describing the writing of those deeply engraved paragraphs—he called it 'chipping every word off the breastbone'. What spellbound me, as I read, was a sensation I have never felt so acutely in any other book. I can only call it the feeling of actuality. The icy feeling of the moment of reality. On every page of Tarka was some phrase, some event, some glimpse, that made the hair move on my head with that feeling. In the confrontations of creature and creature, of creature and object, of creature and fate—he made me feel the pathos of actuality in the natural world. It was the first time I was ever aware of it. But I now know that only truly great writers are ever able to evoke it.

I tried to impose the weird atmosphere of those haunting sentences and episodes on my own doings. And a
world I was already given to completely—my world of
wild creatures in the South Yorkshire countryside—
became a world of Henry's radiant language. In this way,
Tarka put my life under an enchantment that lasted for
years, and that gradually crystallised into an ambition to
write for myself, and to fasten that strange feeling, that
eerie sense of the moment of reality, in my own sentences.
What I had responded to, and been awakened by, was
the poetic intensity of Henry Williamson's vision and
words.

It is not usual to consider him as a poet. But I believe
he was one of the two or three truest poets of his generation. He was different from the others in that he never
published any verse, and I don't know that he even wrote
it. He was dedicated to the presentation of objective
realities in prose—in the tradition of the Tolstoy he loved
so much. But in those early books about wild life, he
created a real poetic mythology. He set it in the actual
world, and he peopled it with actual creatures and men,
but it is in fact an imaginative vision, intensely controlled
at every point by imaginative laws, and it does all the
work of poetry.

That poet of the natural world was the first Henry. The
second Henry I encountered later in a book called
Patriot's Progress. In its way, *Patriot's Progress* is as
phenomenal a piece of writing as *Tarka*. It is a slightly
fictionalised account of Henry Williamson's baptism of
fire in the trench fighting of the First World War. We
see there that spirit of Tarka—a wild supersensitive
creature—entering the dreadful world of Modern History. It is one of the very best records of trench warfare,
and it certainly describes one of the key experiences in
Henry's life.

We now know what a decisive effect that war was to

have on him. In some ways he spent the rest of his days
working out the implications and living out the consequences of what he had lived through there. The
illuminations and shocking revelations of that war against
Germany is at the heart of all his later books. And out of
it came the indignation that drove him along the razor's
edge of his particular brand of political idealism.

The importance to Henry Williamson of his political
ideas can't be ignored, but I don't think it is difficult to
understand when we see how the ideas evolved. He was
not two different writers — an inspired author of nature
stories which everybody loves, on the one hand, and a
political extremist full of unpopular pronouncements on
the other. The whole system was really one system. If one
ignores the superficial errors of judgement he seemed to
make, in trying to adjust his ideas to the practical world
of contemporary politics, and looks instead into the heart
of his books, into the poetic vision which is the dynamo at
the centre, one sees his consistency. At bottom, he worshipped a small group of simple, related things. He gave
them old-fashioned names, often enough, but they were
permanent things, and it seems to me they were real and
good things. They were *the only* real and good things.

First, he worshipped energy. And worshipping energy,
he feared — with a fear that was always ready to become
rage — inertia, disintegration of effort, wilful neglect, any
sort of sloppiness or wasteful exploitation. Even here, we
can see how a keen feeling for a biological law — the
biological struggle against entropy — quickly sprouts its
social and political formulations, with all the attendant
dangers of abstract language. He worshipped natural
creativity — and therefore he rejoiced in anybody who
seemed able to make positive things happen, anybody
who had a practical vision for repairing society, up-
grading craftsmanship, nursing and improving the land.
He worshipped the clear, undistorted spirit of natural

life—and this led him to imagine a society based on natural law, a hierarchic society, a society with a great visionary leader. It seemed to him that he had glimpsed the perfect society in the stable, happy world of some of the big old estates, where discipline, courtesy, tradition, order, community and productive labour flourished in intimate harmony with a natural world that was cherished. And this memory shaped his reaction to the worst side of democracy, the shoddy, traditionless, destructive, urban emptiness that seemed to him to be destroying England, in its ancestral wholeness and richness, and destroying within Englishmen their sense of their own historical character, as effectively as the work of a deliberate enemy. Well, history played some nasty tricks on him, and gave his ideas strange bedfellows, but who is to say that the ideas, in themselves, were wrong? Everything I have described, in the real moral basis of his vision, seems to me good and right for every time and every place. It all springs out of a simple poetic insight into the piety of the natural world, and a passionate concern to take care of it, in which he was quite a long way ahead of his contemporaries. He was a North American Indian sage among Englishmen. Given the extreme vehemence of his nature, it was almost inevitable that he should find himself entangled in other men's misunderstandings. But it is possible now to forget those, and see what he really was talking about!

The third Henry, the Henry who for me at least made everything about Henry Williamson very clear, was the man himself.

I got to know him in his sixties, when I was a little over thirty. Still spellbound by his magical book, albeit quite unconsciously, I had found myself living where I still live, on Tarka's river, the Taw, in the middle of Devon, and pretty soon I made contact with Henry. It seemed very right to see that he too was still spellbound by Tarka,

working in his hut on that patch of territory he bought
with the prizemoney Tarka had won for him long ago.

I remember our first meeting, among a group of young
people, at the house of a friend, and I remember my
astonishment. He had five times the vitality of anybody
there. I remember thinking that he was like a young
man — but of an earlier, more gracious, more confident
age. And throughout our acquaintance that impression
remained, that Henry was really a young man. I imagine
he had changed very little from the time of the First
World War, as if that experience had fixed him, and
preserved him, but with all his activity and freshness and
enthusiasm.

For several years I met him quite often. And gradually
learned my way through his unpredictable moods. And
gradually I understood what I liked about him most of
all. We had terrible arguments about his politics,
wonderful evenings when he told his stories — with what
seemed like microscopically detailed total recall, and a
miraculous ear for dialect, full of wit and drama. And he
was always different, mercurial, emotional, outrageous,
amusing. But in one thing he was constant, and constantly attractive. He was untamed, and he was free.
What D. H. Lawrence would have called his demon was
still in full clear flame. Life and a full share of difficulties
had not humbled him in any way. The tremendous
energy that had driven him through all those long books
was still there, at any moment of the day, a torrent of sur-
prises. His demon had a black side, which gave him his
bad hours, but that was the powerhouse of his writing, it
connected him to the dark world of the elements. It was
the beast on his back that drove him. It was also
Tarka — still wild, alert, open to everything, ready for
anything. It was what pulsed through the best of his
writing, and it was genuinely him, and it was beautiful.
And for that, I, for one, loved him.

Though he's gone now, I can't feel this is a time to mourn. He lived a long life, and he lived it to the end with a gusto and courage and success that few men attain to. He was blessed with an intense vision of the world, and a rare genius for expressing it, which he harvested to the full. He added masterpieces to the literature of his country, and he had fame, and it may be he now has the kind of immortality he would have wanted. What more might we have asked for, for him? I think we should be content to rest in our gratitude, to his Maker, and to him.